The Easy Gourmet

Entrées: The Main Event

SAFEWAY
Canada Safeway Limited 🍁

EILEEN DWILLIES
ANN MERLING
ANGELA NILSEN
EDENA SHELDON

OPUS PRODUCTIONS INC.
VANCOUVER

Published and produced for Canada Safeway Limited by
Opus Productions Inc.
1128 Homer Street
Vancouver, B.C., Canada
V6B 2X6

© Copyright 1989 Opus Productions Inc.

Recipes © Copyright 1989 Eileen Dwillies, Ann Merling,
    Angela Nilsen, Edena Sheldon

Photography © Copyright 1989 Derik Murray

Canadian Cataloguing in Publication Data
    Entrées: The Main Event

            (The Easy Gourmet ; v.1)
            ISBN 0-921926-00-6

            1. Entrées (Cookery). I. Series.
    TX740.E58 1989   641.8'2 C89-091066-9

Corporate Consultant: Norene Kimberley, Palmer Jarvis Advertising
Editor: Mary Schendlinger
Production Manager: Orest Kinasevych
Designers: Tim Kelly, David Counsell
Recipe Coordinator: Eileen Dwillies
Food Stylist: Edena Sheldon
Test Kitchen Manager: Arline Smith
Food Stylist Assistant: Vicky Deering
Test Kitchen Staff: Kathy Alexander, Margaret Bellamy,
        Margot Brown, Joan Cassels, Janet Dwillies, Betsy Filion,
        Rosalind Hill, Arlyne Ledingham, Jennie Meier, Joyce Miller,
        Marge Milne, Alison Sclater

Produced exclusively on the IBM Personal Publishing System and
    IBM PS/2 Personal Systems.

On the cover: Indonesian Chicken Saté with Peanut Sauce (page 80),
Apricot and Orange Glazed "Sticky" Baby Back Ribs (page 56), Creole
BBQ Shrimp Cajun-Style (page 135).

Printed in Canada by Friesen Printers.

"The Easy Gourmet" ™

TABLE OF CONTENTS

About the authors

Eileen Dwillies, whose recipes and articles have been published in *Western Living, Canadian Living* and other Canadian periodicals, also works as a food stylist for print and television, and teaches cooking in her home. Ann Merling is a microwave consultant, teacher and home economist whose extensive experience includes twelve years working with microwave manufacturers and teaching microwave cooking to consumers. Angela Nilsen, a home economist, food stylist and cooking instructor, has written numerous recipes and articles for publications in Europe and North America, and was a food writer with the *Vancouver Sun* for seven years. Edena Sheldon's writing is regularly featured in newspapers, magazines and cookbooks throughout Canada, the U.S. and Europe, including *Bon Appétit* and *Sunset* magazine, and she enjoys an international reputation as a food stylist.

All four authors bring to the recipes their extensive food writing experience, the unique influences of their world travels, and most of all their appreciation of the cooking traditions of Western Canada, where all of them make their home.

About the recipes

Every recipe in this book is carefully and thoroughly kitchen-tested, by a team that includes both new and experienced cooks.

For convenience in shopping and measuring, we "rounded off" in listing the metric quantities of recipe ingredients, so that 1 lb. is converted as 500 g, rather than the technically correct 454 g; 1/2 lb. is shown as 250 g, and so on.

All of the microwave recipes were tested in microwave ovens of 700 watts, so if yours is in the 600 watt range, add 15% to the suggested cooking times. And remember to start with the minimum suggested time and add extra if necessary—every microwave, like every convection oven, is unique.

We used large eggs and whole milk unless specified otherwise, and we used unsalted butter without exception. When you cook with herbs, remember that dried herbs are much more concentrated than fresh ones, so if you substitute dried herbs for fresh, use one-third the amount. When a recipe calls for wine, liqueur, or other alcoholic beverage, there is usually a substitute ingredient listed. There are non-alcoholic cooking wines and liqueurs available, but unless the recipe specifically calls for them, we did not use them, as their salt content is quite high.

4

INTRODUCTION

Welcome to *The Easy Gourmet: Entrées, The Main Event,* the first in an exciting series of four cookbooks that Canada Safeway will present to you throughout this year. Working hand in hand with four of Canada's top food writers, Canada Safeway has developed these books to commemorate its Sixtieth Anniversary with a unique celebration of good taste. Every recipe in *The Easy Gourmet* has been created to take advantage of the wide variety of wholesome foods available at Safeway stores. Each one is kitchen-tested, and all of them are designed for the shopper who wants to cook with ease and entertain with style.

To kick off the series, here is an original collection of tantalizing recipes for meat, poultry, seafood, eggs and cheese. There are plenty of variations on old favourites, as well as some unusual new flavour combinations. Influences from the world's many exotic cooking traditions are to be found here, from the colourful spices and seasonings of the Far East, to the hearty fare of Europe, to the lively concoctions of Central America.

Most of the recipes call for conventional cooking methods, but because so many families have discovered the benefits of the microwave oven in a busy life, there are special microwave recipes sprinkled throughout the book, each marked with the microwave symbol ⓜ.

In many of the recipe introductions, the authors offer serving suggestions and ideas for accompaniments that complement each dish with their colour and flavour. You'll find many tasty, ready-to-go foods at your Safeway store —a baguette or some flaky croissants from the in-store bakery, nutritious prepared salads and colourful, piquant cheeses from the Deli. Each of the specialty departments within the store is staffed by experienced, helpful personnel who are glad to offer advice and information. So go ahead and ask for suggestions on cooking the local catch of the day or selecting a roast for Sunday dinner. If you don't see what you want, just ask the experts!

To make sure you get the best results from the recipes in these pages, here are a few tips for selecting, storing and cooking meat, poultry, seafood, eggs and cheese.

MEAT

Selecting
Safeway's well-stocked meat counters carry year-round favourites as well as a great selection of seasonal meats. Package sizes cater to singles as well as large families, and our staff is always ready to wrap up a special size for you.

Look for meat with "eye appeal"—veal or pork that is rosy pink, beef that is bright red and lamb that is a darker red. Our carefully trimmed meats have only 1/4 inch of fat, which lends juiciness to some cuts: beef, for example, is best with a small amount of marbling throughout.

For roasting, broiling or pan-frying, choose tender cuts (those that have the least muscle) such as steaks, chops and roasts. Less tender cuts —pot roasts and stewing beef—are ideal for slower cooking methods such as braising and stewing.

A pound (about 500 g) of boneless meat such as ground beef, boneless roasts, steaks, stew, or liver, yields about three or four servings, depending on individual appetites. Cuts of meat with some bone in will provide two and a half servings per pound, and meat with plenty of bone, such as spare ribs and oxtails, will yield one to one and a quarter servings per pound.

Cooking
To reduce the amount of fat in the meat, roast or broil it. For roasting, insert a meat thermometer in the centre of the roast and follow the timing guidelines on the thermometer. Remember that roasts continue cooking after they come out of the oven, so let them rest for 15 minutes or so before slicing. Unless the meat is to be served rare, test for doneness by pricking it with a fork and seeing that the juices run clear. This is particularly important with pork.

Storing
Meat purchased from Safeway can be refrigerated in its original package if you plan to use it soon. Stored in the coldest part of the refrigerator, beef, lamb, pork and veal roasts will keep for 2-4 days; steaks, chops, ribs and pork sausages can be stored up to 3 days; stewing meat and variety meats (heart, liver and kidneys) for 2 days. Ground meats should be used by the following day. Smoked and cured meats will keep for a week or two: use the handy "best before" stamp on each package as a guide.

If you are freezing meat, put it in the freezer immediately after you get it home, and wrap it well to prevent "freezer burn." Cover it with moisture-proof freezer quality aluminum foil or plastic wrap. Beef can be frozen for 6-12 months; veal and lamb for 6-9 months; ground beef, veal and lamb for 3-4 months; ground pork for 3 months; pork sausage, bacon and smoked ham for 2 months. To help preserve the texture of the meat, defrost it in the refrigerator rather than at room temperature.

POULTRY
Tender, lean, versatile chicken is certainly the most familiar and popular poultry, but turkey, duck, goose and the tiny Rock Cornish game hens are also available at Safeway. Try game hens done in the microwave, duck roasted with fruity sauces, or chicken stir-fried with exotic flavourings.

Selecting
Cutting up your own poultry is more economical than buying it cut up, but

make sure to consider your family's tastes and the requirements of the recipe, too. For dinner in a hurry, lean turkey cutlets are ideal for quick frying or broiling, and ground turkey is a low-fat substitute for ground beef.

Allow 3-4 ounces (90-125 g) of boneless poultry per serving. Remember that duck and goose has more fat per pound that will reduce when it cooks and yield fewer servings than a chicken or turkey of the same weight.

Cooking
Poultry adapts well to most cooking methods, delicious roasted, broiled, grilled, fried, braised, stewed or poached. Certain types of chicken are best for particular cooking methods: young, tender broiler-fryers can be prepared in any way, whereas the slightly older roasting chicken is meant to be roasted whole. A stewing chicken, larger and more mature, is best simmered gently for a good long time.

To make sure poultry is done, check with a meat thermometer (for roasts), or cut into the flesh and ensure that the juices run clear and the pinkness is gone from the meat.

Storing
Uncooked poultry will keep up to 2 days in the refrigerator, in its original wrapping.

To freeze poultry, wrap it in moisture-proof freezer quality aluminum foil or plastic wrap, and package it in serving-size portions when possible. Whole chickens and turkeys can be stored up to one year in the freezer; game hens and cut-up poultry for 6 months; geese and ducks for 3 months. Defrosting the poultry slowly in the refrigerator will help preserve its texture.

SEAFOOD
To keep Safeway's seafood counters well-stocked with a variety of fish and shellfish, our buyers shop the world. The recipes in *The Easy Gourmet* will give you new inspirations for old favourites, and some ideas for trying the seafoods you haven't yet enjoyed—including recipes that call for convenient frozen and canned fish.

Selecting
Seafood is always best when it is perfectly fresh, or even live from the seafood tanks. The eyes and skin should be shiny and bright, and frozen fish should be frozen solid. If you aren't sure, ask the staff, who are fully trained in handling, storing, and preparing seafood.

Cod, haddock and snapper are good all-purpose fish, whereas prawns and shrimp are usually selected for their attractive colour and distinctive taste. The white fish, such as cod and snapper, have a subtle taste that goes well with the more pungent sauces, and flavourful salmon needs only a simple preparation.

Allow 3/4 lb. (375 g) per person for whole fish; 1/4-1/2 lb. (125-250 g) for fillets or steaks; 1/4 lb. (125 g) for scallops, shrimp meat or crab meat. For oysters and clams in the shell, plan on half a dozen per person.

Storing
Fish is best when it is used right away. Shellfish should be eaten the same day it is purchased; white fish will keep for a day and smoked fish will keep for two days. Fish can be frozen for up to 6 months, but seafood with shells, such as oysters and mussels, should not be frozen.

Cooking
Whether you broil, grill, bake, steam, fry or poach fish, cook it quickly and delicately. Serve it as soon as it turns opaque. All shellfish should be cooked before being served, except oysters and clams which can be eaten raw.

EGGS AND CHEESE
Eggs are favourites for their versatility—they can be whipped up light as a feather for soufflés and they are equally dependable as the binding agent in a batch of crêpes. Like their dairy partner cheese, they are a nutritious protein substitute for meat or fish, at any time of the day.

Selecting
Available in several sizes, Safeway's eggs are Grade A and can be purchased by the half-dozen, dozen or in special family-size packages. Cheese comes in many varieties, all with unique flavours, from all over the world. Choose Edam, Gouda or mild Cheddar for a subtle taste, or for a more sprightly flavour, try Roquefort, Brie or Camembert.

Storing
Always store cheese and eggs in the refrigerator. The softer cheeses are more perishable than the firmer ones, but all should be tightly covered in plastic wrap once they are opened to keep them from drying out. Firm cheeses freeze well for up to 3 months, but softer ones, particularly cream cheese and cottage cheese, lose their texture when frozen. Store cheese in the freezer in blocks no larger than 1 lb. (about 500 g), or it may crumble when it is thawed. Freezing grated cheese is a handy idea—it's always ready for tossing into soups or sauces.

Let refrigerated cheese sit at room temperature for an hour before serving to bring out the maximum flavour.

Cooking
Cook eggs and cheese gently. Eggs will stay moist and soft if they are cooked at a low temperature; cheese stays creamy and flavourful if you cook it slowly and delicately.

MEAT

Nothing satisfies like meat—hearty and filling, it deserves its status as the protein rich "star" of the dinner table. In this section, inspired by the wide variety of beef, pork, veal and lamb at Safeway's meat counters, you will find everything from a classic Prime Rib Roast to tantalizing Apricot and Orange Glazed "Sticky" Baby Back Ribs.

 EPPER STEAK

Long heralded as a favourite (and classic) restaurant dish, Pepper Steak is an entrée for your own special celebration at home! Fresh coarsely-cracked black peppercorns are a must for this dish—just place the peppercorns in a zip-lock plastic bag and pound with a wooden mallet. The rich sauce, a heady reduction of brandy and cream, is quickly finished in the steak skillet. Serve with crunchy shoestring potatoes and crisp watercress. Serves 2.

2	New York steaks, about 1/2 inch (1 cm) thick	2
	freshly cracked black peppercorns	
	salt, if desired	
2 tbsp.	oil	30 mL
4 tbsp.	butter	60 mL
4 tbsp.	brandy or Cognac	60 mL
4 tbsp.	whipping cream	60 mL

Trim the steaks of excess fat. Press the peppercorns into both sides of each steak and salt, if desired. Heat the oil and butter in a medium skillet and cook the steaks over medium-high heat about 3 minutes on each side for rare meat.

Pour in the brandy and immediately light with a match. Stand well back. When the flames die down, lift the meat onto a warm platter and add the whipping cream to the pan. Scrape up the bits of meat drippings and boil the cream for a few minutes over high heat until slightly thickened. Pour the sauce over the steaks and serve immediately.

The Easy Gourmet features a photograph of this recipe on page 17.

S TEAK SANDWICH ON GRILLED SOURDOUGH

For a quick, elegant supper, nothing beats a real steak sandwich, served open-faced on grilled sourdough with an unctuous nap of mustard-spiked pan sauce. Serve with a mound of thick-cut crispy steak fries, a generous garnish of fresh green onions, and a fresh tomato salad. Serves 2.

2	rib-eye or New York steaks, about 1/2 inch (1 cm) thick	2
1 tsp.	olive oil (to film the pan)	5 mL
1/2 tsp.	coarsely ground black pepper or to taste	2 mL
1 tbsp.	*each* olive oil and softened butter	15 mL
1	large clove garlic, halved	1
2	1-inch (2.5 cm) slices sourdough bread, cut from centre of a round 1 lb. (500 g) loaf	2
	salt	
	Mustard Pan Sauce (recipe follows)	

Bring the steaks to room temperature, about 45 minutes. Brush both sides of the meat lightly with the 1 tsp. (5 mL) olive oil, and sprinkle generously with the black pepper.

Combine the 1 tbsp. (15 mL) *each* olive oil and butter. Rub one side of each slice of bread with the cut garlic clove. Brush with the oil-butter mixture. Heat the broiler 5 minutes. "Grill" the bread butter side up 8 inches (20 cm) from the heat source, to a toasty golden brown. Remove it from the broiler and set aside.

Heat a seasoned cast-iron or non-stick skillet over high heat. Sprinkle the bottom of the skillet lightly with salt, and heat for an additional 1 minute. Place the prepared steaks in the hot skillet, and sear 4 minutes per side, turning once for medium-rare. The finished steaks should feel resilient and just slightly firm when pressed. Remove them from the skillet, transfer to a warm platter, and set aside while quickly preparing the Mustard Pan Sauce.

MUSTARD PAN SAUCE

2 tbsp.	butter	30 mL
3 tbsp.	minced shallots	45 mL
1 tbsp.	Worcestershire sauce	15 mL
1 tbsp.	brandy or whiskey (optional)	15 mL
1/2 cup	whipping cream	125 mL
1 tbsp.	Dijon-style mustard	15 mL
1 tbsp.	grainy mustard	15 mL
	salt and pepper to taste	
	green onions for garnish	

Wipe the hot skillet clean, leaving 1 tbsp. (15 mL) of the drippings. Add the butter to the skillet, heat to bubbly and add the minced shallots. Sauté, stirring, until pale golden, 2-3 minutes. Add the Worcestershire sauce, brandy (or whiskey) and heat over high heat 2 minutes to evaporate. Stir in the cream. Cook the sauce, stirring, until it is bubbly and thickened. Remove sauce from the heat, whisk in the two mustards, season with salt and pepper to taste.

To assemble sandwiches: Place the warm bread on warmed plates, top each with one hot steak, and nap steaks with the warm sauce. Garnish with green onions, and serve at once.

The Easy Gourmet features a photograph of this recipe on page 17.

GINGER BEEF STIR-FRY

This spicy Chinese stir-fry dish of slivered marinated beef and steamed Oriental vegetables makes for a lovely one-dish presentation with fluffy steamed rice. Serve with cold beer or traditional tea, and finish with a bowl of Mandarin oranges and fortune cookies. Serves 4.

1 lb.	beef top sirloin steak	500 g
1 tbsp.	*each* cornstarch, vegetable oil and soy sauce	15 mL
2 tbsp.	vegetable oil, for frying	30 mL
2	cloves garlic, crushed	2
1 tbsp.	coarsely grated fresh ginger	15 mL
1/2 cup	beef stock or bouillon	125 mL
2 tbsp.	soy sauce	30 mL
1/2 tsp.	sugar	2 mL
5	green onions, sliced diagonally	5
2 tbsp.	chopped fresh cilantro	30 mL
4 cups	diagonally sliced bok choy (leaves and white stem)	1 L
2 cups (about 2 oz.)	fresh bean sprouts, rinsed	500 mL (about 50 g)
1 1/2 cups	long-grain rice, cooked	375 mL
1 tbsp.	toasted sesame seeds	15 mL

Slice the beef into thin strips, about 3 inches (7.5 cm) long and 3/4 inch (2 cm) wide. In a medium bowl, combine the cornstarch, 1 tbsp. (15 mL) of vegetable oil and soy sauce and toss in the beef to coat well. Cover with plastic wrap and marinate in the refrigerator for 1 hour.

Heat the 2 tbsp. (30 mL) oil in a wok or large skillet and sauté the garlic and ginger over medium heat for 1 minute. Turn the heat to high and fry the beef, stirring constantly to break it up, about 4 minutes or until cooked. Turn the heat to low and stir in the stock, soy sauce and sugar. Add the green onions and cilantro and cook, stirring, 1 minute. Keep warm.

Meanwhile, steam the bok choy until tender-crisp, about 5 minutes, adding the bean sprouts on top for the last 30 seconds to heat through.

To serve, place the rice in a warm 2 quart (2 L) shallow casserole dish. Top with the bok choy and bean sprouts. Pour the beef and sauce over top and sprinkle with sesame seeds.

STEAK AND KIDNEY PIE

Traditional British cooking conjures up visions of steak and kidney pie. True comfort food, it relies on gentle cooking to bring out the natural taste of the meats. It is best to make the filling a day ahead so the flavours can really develop. Then top it with a puffy pie crust and serve with creamed potatoes and crisp steamed vegetables. Serves 6.

1 1/2 lbs.	stew beef, trimmed and cut in 1 inch (2.5 cm) cubes	750 g
1/2 lb.	beef kidney, cut in small pieces with core removed	250 g
4 tbsp.	all-purpose flour	60 mL
1/2 tsp.	salt	2 mL
1/4 tsp.	pepper	1 mL
2 tbsp.	vegetable oil	30 mL
1	medium onion, sliced	1
1	beef bouillon cube, dissolved in 1 cup (250 mL) boiling water	1
1/4 lb.	mushrooms, quartered	125 g
1	7 1/2 oz. (215 g) pkg. frozen puff pastry, thawed	1
	beaten egg or milk, for glazing	

Heat the oven to 325°F (160°C).

In a large bowl, toss the meat, kidney, flour, salt and pepper until the meat is well coated. Heat the oil in large saucepan and fry the onion over medium heat until soft but not brown. Add the meat and kidney and cook, stirring, over high heat, about 4 minutes or until the meat loses its raw look. Pour in the bouillon and bring to a boil, stirring until it thickens. Stir in the mushrooms. Transfer the mixture to a casserole dish, cover and bake about 2 1/2 hours, stirring once or twice, until the meat is tender. Remove it from the oven, taste to check seasoning and place the meat and just enough gravy to cover the meat, into a 1 quart (1 L) oval pie dish with a rim. The dish will be quite full. (Reserve any extra gravy for serving with the pie.) Refrigerate overnight or allow to cool, covered.

Before serving, heat the oven to 425°F (220°C). Roll out the pastry to an oval 1 inch (2.5 cm) larger all around than the pie dish. Cut off a narrow strip (the same width as the rim of the dish) from the pastry edge. Moisten the rim of the dish with water and line it with the pastry strip. Moisten the strip and cover the meat filling with the remaining pastry oval, trimming if necessary and pressing the edges to seal. Flute the edges. Cut a small vent in the centre of the pastry for steam to escape. Decorate the pie with pastry leaves if desired.

Glaze the top with beaten egg or milk and bake, on a cookie sheet, until the pastry is puffed and golden, about 30-35 minutes. Heat the reserved gravy in a small pan to accompany the pie.

OUISA'S GOULASH

Nothing warms the hearts of your loved ones like a slowly simmered stew, and the piquant seasonings in this one make it perfectly memorable. It reheats beautifully, so make it ahead, then serve it hot with steamy buttered noodles. Serves 4.

1 lb.	onions, chopped	500 g
3 tbsp.	oil or butter	45 mL
1	clove garlic, crushed	1
2 tbsp.	paprika	30 mL
1 tsp.	marjoram	5 mL
1 tsp.	caraway seeds (optional)	5 mL
2 lbs.	stew beef, cubed	1 kg
pinch	*each* salt and pepper	pinch
2	10 oz. (284 mL) cans beef broth or stock	2
	bread crumbs (optional)	

Fry the onion in the oil until softened. Then mix in the garlic, paprika, marjoram and caraway. Add the meat and stir well. Cook over medium-high heat until the meat browns. Add 1 can of beef broth, reduce the heat and simmer until the liquid is almost gone. Season to taste. Add the second can of broth and continue simmering until liquid is almost gone. Stir in bread crumbs to thicken as necessary.

CHINESE ORANGE-BEEF AND GINGER CASSEROLE

Long, slow cooking gives a melt-in-the-mouth taste to this Oriental beef casserole. The fragrant scent of orange and the tang of fresh ginger mingle together as it simmers, and the only accompaniment you need is fluffy boiled rice. Serves 4.

1 lb.	stew beef, trimmed of fat	500 g
	oil, for frying	
1	medium onion, peeled and thinly sliced	1
3 tbsp.	soy sauce	45 mL
2 tbsp.	Chinese cooking wine	30 mL
4	thin slices of fresh ginger, peeled	4
1 tsp.	sugar	5 mL
1 3/4 cups	water	425 mL
1	orange	1
1/4 lb.	snow peas, trimmed	125 g
1	7 oz. (225 mL) can sliced bamboo shoots, drained	1

Heat the oven to 325°F (160°C).

Cut the beef into 1-inch (2.5 cm) cubes. Pour enough oil into a medium-sized, heavy-based pan to come 1/2 inch (1 cm) up the sides. Heat the oil to 400°F (200°C) and fry the meat for 4 minutes. Remove the meat with a slotted spoon and place it in a saucepan. Pour in enough boiling water to cover the meat, bring to a boil and boil for 2 minutes. Drain off the water and place the beef in a 1 1/2 quart (1.5 L) deep casserole dish. Add the onion, soy sauce, cooking wine, ginger, sugar and water.

Cut four 1-inch (2.5 cm) wide strips of orange peel from the orange, removing any pith. Stir into the casserole. Remove all remaining peel and pith from the orange, slice the flesh and reserve.

Cover the casserole and bake for 3 1/2 hours, stirring occasionally. Add the snow peas, bamboo shoots and reserved orange slices during the last 5 minutes of cooking time. Serve hot with rice or buttered noodles.

Opposite: (Top to bottom) Pepper Steak (page 9); Steak Sandwich on Grilled Sourdough (page 10).

SHEPHERD'S PIE

Sometimes called cottage pie, this family favourite is a great way to use up the leftovers from a roast beef dinner. And the recipe is easily doubled or even tripled if you're cooking for a crowd. A hearty meal in a dish, this entreé needs only a crisp, curly green salad for accompaniment. Serves 6.

2 cups	cold cooked beef, cut into bite-sized pieces, minced or shredded	500 mL
2 cups	cooked mixed vegetables	500 mL
1/2 - 1 cup	leftover gravy (if none available, see note below)	125 - 250 mL
2 tbsp.	tomato paste	30 mL
1 tsp.	Worcestershire sauce	5 mL
	salt and pepper to taste	
3	potatoes, cooked and mashed, or enough to cover the top of the hash to a depth of 1 inch (2.5 cm)	3

Heat the oven to 400°F (200°C). Grease a 1 1/2-2 quart (1.5-2 L) baking dish or casserole.

In a large bowl, mix together all the ingredients except the mashed potatoes. Taste and adjust the seasonings. Place the mixture in the casserole dish and cover with the mashed potatoes, forming peaks and valleys as you would do with a meringue topping. Bake until bubbly and golden brown, about 20-30 minutes.

Note: Here is a quick, simple recipe for gravy if you don't have any left over. In a jar with a lid, place 2 tbsp. (30 mL) flour and 1/2 cup (125 mL) beef stock or canned broth. Cover the jar and shake until the flour is absorbed into the stock. Pour it into a small saucepan and heat to boiling, stirring in more stock to make a medium-thick gravy. Taste and add a few drops of beef bovril until it reaches the flavour you desire.

MEXICAN BEEF FAJITAS WITH CONDIMENTS

*Fajitas (pronounced fah-*hee-tass*) have become wildly popular in the past few years—"do it yourself" soft tacos or burritos filled with grilled meat and condiments. Fajitas make perfect family or entertaining fare; simple to do, deliciously addictive, and most of all—fun! Serve with warmed flour or corn tortillas, a bowl of avocado guacamole (homemade or frozen, thawed), sour cream, and fresh tomato salsa. Offer a warmed pot of refried beans and a pitcher of cold beer or limeade. Serves 6-8.*

2 lbs.	sirloin steak	1 kg
1/2 cup	fresh lime juice	125 mL
4 tbsp.	fresh lemon juice	60 mL
1/3 cup	salad oil	75 mL
3	large cloves garlic, minced	3
1 tsp.	*each* dried oregano and ground cumin	5 mL
1/2 tsp.	*each* black pepper and chili powder	2 mL
3	onions, halved lengthwise, peeled intact	3
12	green onions, rinsed	12

Slice the steak crosswise into 12-inch (30 cm) strips. Place in a shallow glass or crockery dish. Combine the lime juice, lemon juice, oil, garlic, oregano, cumin, black pepper and chili powder. Pour this mixture over the meat, turning to coat, and add the onions to the marinade cut side down. Cover and refrigerate 4-6 hours, turning the meat several times.

Heat the barbecue coals to hot, about 1 hour. Grill the meat and the onion halves 4 inches (10 cm) from the heat source, basting with the marinade and turning once. Cook the meat about 6-8 minutes altogether for rare or medium-rare. Cook the onions until tender and slightly golden brown. Remove the meat and onions from the grill. Dip the green onions in the marinade and grill 3-4 minutes until tender and slightly charred. Remove them from the grill.

To serve, thinly slice the meat across the grain. Separate the onions into sections. Heat tortillas on the grill 25 seconds to soften, as needed. Offer suggested condiments (below).

Place several slices of meat down the centre of a softened tortilla. Add a spoonful of warmed beans, if desired. Top with guacamole, sour cream and salsa, and tuck in one long scallion. Add a sprig or two of fresh cilantro. Fold up the bottom, and roll the sides to enclose the filling. Eat and enjoy.

Note: This recipe is delicious broiled, as well as barbecued. Broil the meat on a shallow pan 3 inches (7.5 cm) from the heat source, turning once, about 6-7 minutes total cooking time for rare to medium-rare. Broil onions 6 inches (15 cm) from the heat source until golden brown. Chicken may also be used; follow the recipe exactly, substituting boneless breast of chicken.

Suggested Condiments:

12-18	flour or corn tortillas, heated	12-18
1	14 oz. (398 mL) can refried beans, heated	1
2 cups	fresh tomato salsa	500 mL
2 cups	avocado guacamole (your favourite recipe, or frozen product, thawed)	500 mL
1 cup	sour cream	250 mL
	fresh cilantro sprigs	

OLD WORLD CALVES LIVER WITH BACON AND APPLES

This delicate version of calves liver features slices fried to a rosy turn and served with crispy bacon, fried onions, and fragrant apple rings flavoured with cinnamon. Serves 2.

4	slices bacon	4
3 tbsp.	*each* unsalted butter and	45 mL
	bacon drippings	
8 oz.	calves liver, thinly sliced and patted dry	250 g
	all-purpose flour	
	salt and pepper to taste	
1	large onion, thinly sliced	1
1 tsp.	brown sugar	5 mL
2	small apples, cored and peeled	2
2 tbsp.	*each* unsalted butter and sugar	30 mL
2 tsp.	ground cinnamon	10 mL
	juice and rind of 1 lemon	

Fry the bacon until crispy brown. Remove and keep warm. Add 1 tbsp. (15 mL) of the butter to the skillet and heat on medium-high until bubbly. Dredge the liver in flour; shake off the excess. Quickly sauté the liver in the hot drippings mixture for 2-3 minutes on each side, until crusty and brown on the outside, rosy pink on the inside. Season with salt and pepper. Remove it from the skillet, transfer it to a platter and keep warm.

Wipe the skillet clean, and add 2 tbsp. (30 mL) butter. Heat over medium-high heat, add the onion and sugar, and sauté 5-7 minutes until limp and golden. Scatter the onions over the pan.

Slice the apples into 1/2 inch (1 cm) thick rings. Heat the remaining 2 tbsp. (30 mL) butter to foaming in a large non-stick skillet. Add the apple rings, and fry over medium-high heat until golden. Sprinkle with the sugar and cinnamon, and fry until dark golden and carmelized. Sprinkle with lemon juice and rind, and fry 2 minutes or until all the juices are absorbed. Serve hot or warm.

SOUTHWEST SHORT RIBS

This succulent version of meaty short ribs is Southwest-inspired, owing to the unique marinade that uses prepared red salsa. Serve with steamed white rice, hearty black beans, fresh lime wedges to squeeze over the ribs, and a colourful and cooling salad of fresh avocado, navel oranges, red onions and scallions dressed in a vinaigrette. Offer crusty corn muffins or tortillas in a pretty basket. Serves 6-8.

6 lbs.	meaty beef short ribs, cracked	3 kg
1 cup	dry red wine (or 1/2 cup (125 mL) *each* red wine vinegar and water combined)	250 mL
1 cup	red chili *salsa* (bottled or fresh from the deli)	250 mL
2 tsp.	*each* ground cumin, cloves and oregano	10 mL
1 tsp.	ground allspice	5 mL
1 tsp.	ground black pepper	5 mL
4 tbsp.	corn oil	60 mL
2 tbsp.	salt	30 mL
2	cloves garlic, minced	2
3 tbsp.	brown sugar, packed	45 mL
	crisp cilantro for garnish	

Place the short ribs in a deep crockery or glass bowl. Stir together the wine, *salsa,* cumin, allspice, pepper, corn oil, salt, garlic and brown sugar. Pour the marinade over the ribs, toss to coat, and cover with plastic wrap. Refrigerate 6 hours or overnight, turning the meat several times in the marinade.

Heat outdoor barbecue coals to medium-hot, about 35 minutes. Place the grill 4-6 inches (10-15 cm) above coals. Oil the grill. Remove the ribs from the marinade and drain briefly. Place them on the grill, cover with hood with drafts *open*, and cook 35-40 minutes. Turn and baste with marinade every 10 minutes. The finished ribs should be medium-rare or medium, with a crusty brown exterior.

Remove the ribs from the grill and serve them sizzling hot. Garnish the platter of ribs with fresh cilantro and offer additional *salsa* on the side.

PRIME RIB ROAST WITH YORKSHIRE PUDDING

A standing prime rib of beef roast is the finest of all meats—worth every penny, so splurge in the grand manner! Serve it crusty and browned on the outside, juicy and rare on the inside, and accompany with crispy Yorkshire Pudding, creamed corn, fresh spinach, and a creamy horseradish sauce. Serves 6.

3 lbs.	prime rib roast, well tied, or boned, rolled and tied	1.5 kg

Heat the oven to 350°F (180°C) and place the roast, rib side down, in a shallow pan. Insert a meat thermometer into the thickest part of the roast, making sure the tip does not touch a bone.

For very rare, allow 15-17 minutes per pound (500 g), 130°F (55°C) on the thermometer. For medium rare, allow 16-19 minutes per pound, 140°F (60°C) on the thermometer. For well done, allow 20-30 minutes per pound, 165°F (75°C) on the thermometer.

When the roast is done, remove it from the oven and let it rest for 20 minutes. This allows the juices to settle and makes carving much easier. Less juice will run out onto the platter and the meat will be more succulent.

Skim off the fat for the Yorkshire Puddings. The puddings will bake in a hot oven while the roast rests.

To carve, stand the roast on its side so that the ribs are to your left. Holding the meat firmly with a fork, cut along the bone to a depth of 2 or 3 inches (5-7.5 cm), then cut in slices across the top of the roast.

YORKSHIRE PUDDINGS

1 cup	milk, at room temperature	250 mL
1 cup	all-purpose flour	250 mL
3	large eggs, at room temperature	3
pinch	salt	pinch
	fat from the roast or butter or shortening for greasing pan	

In a medium bowl, beat together the milk, flour, eggs and salt. Set aside until it reaches room temperature.

Heat the oven to 450°F (230°C). Generously grease 12 medium muffin cups or one 8 inch (20 cm) pan with 2 inch (5 cm) sides. Place the pan in the oven to heat.

Pour the batter into the hot pan. Bake until well puffed and very dark golden brown, 15-20 minutes.. Serve immediately.

 ERB-CRUSTED STANDING RIB ROAST

This is a delicious way to serve a standing rib roast or baron of beef—crusty with salt and herbs on the outside, juicy and rosy-rare on the inside. Oven-roasted potatoes and fresh creamed spinach flavoured with nutmeg complete this dinner menu. Serves 8-10.

1	4-5 rib standing rib beef roast (bones in)	1
1/2 cup	coarse salt	125 mL
1 tbsp.	*each* dried thyme, basil, rosemary and coarse black pepper	15 mL

Bring the roast to room temperature (about 1 hour). Combine the salt and herbs in a small bowl. Moisten the fat with water (a water-sprayer is ideal). With your hands, crust the fat all over with the herbed-salt mixture. Do not season the flesh-ends of the roast. Heat the oven to 350°F (180°C).

Place the seasoned roast, bones down (this serves as the roast's own roasting rack) in a parchment-lined shallow roasting pan. Allow 17-18 minutes per pound (500 g) for rare, or 125°F (50°C) on a meat thermometer. The meat will continue to cook after it is removed from the oven.

Remove the roast from the oven, and allow it to rest 15-20 minutes before carving. This will allow the roast to absorb all the juices, and will facilitate carving. Carve the roast into 1/2 inch (1 cm) thick slices, serving the crusty roasted bones to those who speak up first!

ROLLED PRIME RIB ROAST WITH MADEIRA SAUCE

Everyone loves prime rib. Serve this one with creamy mashed potatoes and a medley of microwave-steamed vegetables, and watch your family or guests come back for more. Make sure to cook the meat slowly—the results are worth the extra few minutes. Serves 8.

1	2-3 lb. (1-1.5 kg) prime rib roast, boned and rolled	1
1	medium onion, thinly sliced	1
1	clove garlic, crushed	1
1/2 tsp.	salt	2 mL
1/2 tsp.	freshly ground black pepper	2 mL

Sauce:

1	10 oz. (284 mL) can condensed beef broth	1
1/4 tsp.	pepper	1 mL
4 tbsp.	Madeira wine	60 mL

Unroll the beef and lay it fat side down.

Place the onion, garlic, salt and pepper in a small microproof dish. Cover and microwave on HIGH 100% power 2-3 minutes until the onion is soft. Spread the mixture evenly over the meat. Re-roll and tie the beef.

Place the meat seam side down on a microproof roasting rack. Cover with waxed paper and microwave on MEDIUM HIGH 70% power, allowing 9-11 minutes per pound (500 g) for rare, 11-13 minutes per pound (500 g) for medium, 13-15 minutes per pound (500 g) for well done.

Halfway through the required cooking time remove the waxed paper. Baste the meat with drippings and then drain off any excess fat from the dish. Shield the ends of the roast with foil if necessary. Continue to microwave on MEDIUM HIGH 70% power, uncovered, for the remaining cooking time.

Remove the meat from the roasting rack onto a platter. Cover with foil and let stand 10-15 minutes.

To make the sauce, combine all ingredients in a 4-cup (1 L) microproof measure. Microwave on HIGH 100% power to bring it to a boil, reduce to MEDIUM LOW 30% power and allow to simmer 10 minutes—do not boil.

To serve, slice the roast and serve it with the sauce.

CLASSIC SPAGHETTI AND MEATBALLS

Who can turn down a heaping plate of spaghetti topped with a ladleful of rich, red marinara sauce—made even better with plump, succulent spicy meatballs! Add a crusty, hot loaf of garlic bread, a crisp green salad with a zesty vinaigrette and a bowl of Mediterranean olives and you have a dinner to please the family or to turn a party into a feast. Serves 6.

MARINARA SAUCE

4 tbsp.	olive oil	60 mL
2	cloves garlic, minced	2
1 cup	finely diced onion	250 mL
1	28 oz. (796 mL) can tomato pureé	1
1 tbsp.	red wine vinegar	15 mL
1 tbsp.	sugar	15 mL
2/3 cup	dry red wine, beef stock or water	150 mL
2 tsp.	*each* dried oregano and basil	10 mL
1 tsp.	salt	5 mL
1/2 tsp.	pepper	2 mL
1/3 cup	minced fresh parsley	75 mL

Heat the olive oil in a large saucepan over medium-high heat. Add the garlic and onion, and sauté, stirring, until pale golden and softened. Stir in the tomato purée, vinegar and sugar and heat until bubbly, about 2-3 minutes, to evaporate the vinegar. Add the wine, oregano, basil, salt and pepper. Bring to a simmer, partially cover, and cook the sauce over low heat 30 minutes to blend flavours and to thicken. Stir in the parsley, and simmer for an additional 5 minutes. Set aside.

CLASSIC MEATBALLS SOUTHERN-STYLE

1 1/2 lbs.	regular ground beef	750 g
4	slices bacon, finely minced or ground	4
3/4 cup	fresh bread crumbs	175 mL
2	eggs, slightly beaten	2
1 1/2 cups	freshly grated Parmesan cheese	375 mL
1	small onion, finely minced	1
1 tbsp.	finely grated lemon rind	15 mL
4 tbsp.	minced fresh parsley	60 mL
1 tbsp. + 2 tsp.	salt	25 mL
2 tsp.	*each* dried oregano and basil	10 mL
1/2 tsp.	*each* ground allspice and black pepper	2 mL
6 tbsp.	olive oil	90 mL
1 lb.	spaghetti or spaghettini	500 g

In a large mixing bowl, lightly combine the ground beef, bacon, bread crumbs, eggs, 1/2 cup (125 mL) of the Parmesan cheese, onion, lemon rind, parsley, salt, oregano, basil, allspice and black pepper. Mix gently but thoroughly. Loosely cover the mixture, and refrigerate several hours (or overnight) to blend the flavours.

Form the mixture into round 1 1/4 inch (3 cm) meatballs (moisten your hands first to prevent the mixture from sticking to them). Heat 3 tbsp. (45 mL) of the olive oil in a very large non-stick skillet over medium-high heat. Fry the meatballs (do not crowd), shaking the pan frequently to keep the meatballs round, until they are golden brown on all sides.

Add the meatballs to the prepared marinara sauce, cover, and simmer over low heat 45 minutes.

Meanwhile, cook the spaghetti *al dente* (slightly firm to the bite) in 6 quarts (6 L) boiling water with 1 tbsp. (15 mL) *each* of the salt and olive oil. Drain the spaghetti, and in a large crockery bowl toss it hot with 2 tbsp. (30 mL) of the olive oil and 1 cup (250 mL) of the warmed sauce. Serve the spaghetti on warmed plates, topping it with the remaining sauce and the meatballs. Serve at once, piping hot, and pass the remaining Parmesan cheese.

MEXICAN STUFFED BEEF BURGERS

These south-of-the-border inspired beef burgers reveal a delicious savoury filling of melted Monterey jack cheese and roasted whole chiles. Tuck them into toasted sesame seed burger buns that have been grilled with spicy chili-mayonnaise. Slather with an array of Mexican condiments, and enjoy! Serves 4-6.

1 1/2 lbs.	regular ground beef	750 g
1/2 cup	finely sliced green onion	125 mL
1/3 cup	*each* minced green bell pepper and pitted black olives	75 mL
1/2 cup	bottled red taco sauce	125 mL
1/2 tsp.	ground cumin	2 mL
1 tsp.	*each* dried oregano, salt and black pepper	5 mL
1	3 1/2 oz. (110 g) can roasted whole green chiles, drained, split, seeded and flattened	1
6 oz.	Monterey jack cheese, coarsely grated	200 g
4-6	sesame seed hamburger buns	4-6
4 tbsp.	mayonnaise	60 mL
1 tsp.	chili powder	5 mL
	suggested condiments (see below)	

Lightly combine the ground beef, green onion, green pepper, black olives, taco sauce, cumin, oregano, salt and pepper. Knead 1-2 minutes to bind the mixture together. Divide the mixture into 8-12 equal portions. With moistened hands, gently shape each portion into a flattened patty.

Spread the prepared chiles on half of the patties, leaving a 1 inch (2.5 cm) border all around. Top the chiles with the grated cheese. Cover with the remaining patties, pressing the edges to enclose the filling. Chill the burgers on a flat plate, uncovered, for 1 hour to firm. Combine the mayonnaise and chili powder, and spread on the cut sides of the buns. Grill the burgers over charcoal or under the broiler on an oiled rack or pan 4 inches (10 cm) from the heat source. Sear 4 minutes on the first side, turn, and sear 4 minutes on the other side for medium-rare. Remove the burgers from the heat, and allow to set 3-4 minutes for the juices to absorb. Grill the buns, mayonnaise side up, 4 inches (10 cm) from the heat source until crispy and golden brown.

Serve the burgers hot and crusty on toasted buns at once, and pass the condiments.

Suggested Condiments: guacamole (your own or frozen, thawed), sour cream, sliced black olives, bottled taco sauce, crisp bacon slices, thin rounds of onion, shredded romaine lettuce, sliced tomatoes.

ROQUEFORT-STUFFED BEEF BURGERS

These party-fare burgers deluxe *get a surprise filling of creamy Roquefort—savoury and delicious tucked inside a toasty grilled bun with all the traditional condiments. Serve with cold beer or a pitcher of iced tea, and a big bowl of homemade french-style steak fries. Serves 4-6.*

1 1/2 lbs.	regular ground beef	750 g
1 tbsp.	Worcestershire sauce	15 mL
1/3 cup	finely minced onion	75 mL
1	large clove garlic, minced	1
1 tsp.	*each* salt and black pepper	5 mL
4 oz.	Roquefort or blue cheese, softened	125 g
4 oz.	butter, softened	125 g
4	Kaiser-style rolls, cut open	4
4 tbsp.	mayonnaise	60 mL

Lightly combine the ground beef, Worcestershire sauce, onion, garlic, salt and pepper. Divide into 8-12 equal portions. With moistened hands, gently form each portion into a flattened patty.

Cream together the cheese and butter. Divide it among 4-6 (half) of the patties, placing in the centre of the patty with a 1-inch (2.5 cm) border all around. Top each filled patty with another patty, pressing to seal the edges and enclose the filling. Chill the burgers for 1 hour on a flat plate, uncovered, to firm. Spread mayonnaise on the inside of both the top and bottom halves of the buns. Grill the burgers over charcoal, or broil them on an oiled rack or pan 4 inches (10 cm) from the heat source. Sear 4 minutes on the first side, turn, and sear 4 minutes on the other side for medium-rare. Remove burgers from heat, and allow them to rest 3-4 minutes for the juices to be absorbed. Grill the buns, mayonnaise side up, 4 inches (10 cm) from the heat source until crispy and golden brown.

Serve the burgers hot and crusty on toasted buns and pass the condiments.

Suggested Condiments: Thin rounds of red onion, slices of beefsteak tomatoes, thin cucumber slices, leaf lettuce, grainy mustard, honey mustard.

MEATBALLS STROGANOFF

Quick, easy, tasty—the perfect answer for a hearty family dinner! Try this dish with buttered noodles and sweet and sour red cabbage for a soul-satisfying meal on a rainy winter evening. Serves 4.

1 lb.	lean ground beef	500 g
1	egg, beaten	1
3/4 cup	fresh bread crumbs	175 mL
4 tbsp.	wheat germ	60 mL
1/2 tsp.	dried basil	2 mL
1/4 tsp.	freshly ground black pepper	1 mL
1	10 oz. (284 mL) can golden mushroom soup	1
1/2 cup	sour cream	125 mL
3 tbsp.	chopped parsley	45 mL
2 tbsp.	red wine (optional)	30 mL

Combine the meat with the sour cream, egg, bread crumbs, wheat germ, basil, pepper, 4 tbsp. (60 mL) of the soup, 4 tbsp. (60 mL) of the sour cream and 2 tbsp. (30 mL) of the parsley. Mix well and shape into even-sized balls about 1 1/2 inches (3.5 cm) in diameter. Arrange the balls in a circle on a microproof plate. Cover with waxed paper and microwave on MEDIUM 50% power 4-6 minutes until cooked. Halfway through the cooking time, rotate each meatball a half turn. Let stand, covered.

Combine the remaining soup, sour cream and wine in a 2-cup (500 mL) microproof measure. Microwave on MEDIUM 50% power 2-5 minutes until heated through, stirring once or twice during the cooking time.

To serve, place the meatballs on a serving platter and top with sauce and reserved chopped parsley.

FAR EAST CASSEROLE

Inspired by the flavours of the Orient, this quick, colourful, nutritious casserole freezes so well you'll want to make lots of it for later. Just add a simple tossed salad and a loaf of crusty bread. Serves 5.

1 lb.	lean ground beef	500 g
4 tbsp.	chopped celery	60 mL
4 tbsp.	chopped onion	60 mL
4 tbsp.	chopped green bell pepper	60 mL
1 cup + 1 1/2 tbsp.	water	275 mL
1 1/2 tbsp.	cornstarch	25 mL
1 tsp.	sugar	5 mL
1 tsp.	chopped fresh ginger *or*	5 mL
1/4 tsp.	ground ginger (or to taste)	1 mL
4 tbsp.	teriyaki sauce	60 mL
1	7 oz. (225 mL) can bamboo shoots, drained	1
1	8 oz. (250 g) pkg. frozen snow peas	1
1	8 oz. (250 g) pkg. frozen peas	1
5 cups	chow mein noodles	1.25 L

In a medium skillet, over medium-high heat, cook the ground beef, celery, onion and green pepper until the meat is browned. Drain off any fat. Add 1 cup (250 mL) of the water and bring the mixture to boiling. In a small bowl, combine the cornstarch, sugar and ginger. Blend in the teriyaki sauce and the remaining 1 1/2 tbsp. (25 mL) water. Add the teriyaki mixture to the beef mixture. Cook and stir until thickened and bubbly.

Stir in the bamboo shoots, snow peas and peas. Simmer until the mixture is heated through and the vegetables are tender, about 5 minutes. Ladle over mounds of chow mein noodles on a warmed platter or serving plates.

To freeze, stop after you stir in the vegetables, turn into freezer containers, seal and freeze. Bake the frozen mixture at 400°F (200°C) for 1 1/2 hours or until bubbling.

Opposite: Garlic and Herbed Roast Leg of Lamb (page 59).

ITALIAN SAUSAGES WITH "TRI-COLORE" PEPPERS

This dish takes full advantage of the lush colourful peppers available in our produce departments today. Vibrant reds, yellows, oranges and even purple join the more common green pepper. Serve juicy and sizzling hot over an al dente robust pasta such as rigatoni, penne or ziti. Add a green salad and a crisp loaf of Italian bread—and you have a feast for everyone. Serves 4-6.

8-12	fresh Italian sausages, about 2 lbs. (1kg)	8-12
8	assorted bell peppers (select from red, orange, yellow and green)	8
1/2 cup + 2 tbsp.	olive oil	155 mL
2	cloves garlic, peeled and slivered	2
2 tsp.	salt to taste	10 mL
1 tbsp.	sugar	15 mL
4 tbsp.	red wine vinegar	60 mL
2 tbsp.	capers, drained	30 mL
	minced fresh parsley	
3/4 lb.	pasta, cooked *al dente*, tossed with 4 tbsp. (60 mL) olive oil and seasoned to taste with salt and pepper	375 g

Prick the sausages on all sides with a fork. Blanch in simmering water 8 minutes until the sausages just turn opaque. Drain them completely and pat dry. Heat 2 tbsp. (30 mL) of the olive oil in a large non-stick skillet over high heat. Brown them on all sides, shaking the pan. Reduce heat to medium, and cook the sausages slowly, partially covered, until cooked through, about 20 minutes. Keep warm.

Halve, seed, de-rib and cut the peppers into 1/2-inch (1 cm) strips. Add the remaining 1/2 cup (125 mL) olive oil to the bottom of a very large skillet or wok. Heat over medium-high heat, add the garlic, and sauté 1 minute . Add the peppers, toss and heat 5 minutes, and reduce the heat to medium. Sauté the peppers until just tender. Add the salt and sugar and cook 2 minutes. Add the vinegar and capers and cook 2 minutes more. Combine the hot peppers with the cooked sausages, sprinkle with minced parsley, and serve over piping hot pasta with all the pan juices.

The Easy Gourmet features a photograph of this recipe on page 53.

GROUND VEAL AND GREEN PEPPERCORN TERRINE

This very "up-scale" meat loaf is delicious served warm from the oven for supper—and (perhaps) even better served in very thin slices, chilled, for sandwiches the following day. Either way, try it! Serve it for dinner with a hearty rice dish, a fresh green vegetable, and sugar-glazed fresh field carrots. In a sandwich, a slather of honey-mustard and leaf lettuce does the trick. Makes one large 2 lb. (1 kg) meat loaf. Serves 6-8.

2 lbs.	ground veal	1 kg
2	eggs, slightly beaten	2
1	large onion, finely minced	1
2/3 cup	bread crumbs	150 mL
1/3 cup	Marsala or dry sherry	75 mL
1 tsp.	*each* salt, black pepper, and dried thyme	5 mL
3 tbsp.	green peppercorns, drained (imported from Madagascar, packed in brine; with condiments)	45 mL
1/2 cup + 2 tbsp.	finely grated Parmesan cheese	155 mL
1/3 cup	tomato sauce	75 mL
2 tbsp.	brown sugar	30 mL

In a large electric mixer fitted with a dough-hook, gently mix together the veal, eggs, onion, bread crumbs, Marsala (or sherry), salt, pepper, thyme, green peppercorns and 1/2 cup (125 mL) of the Parmesan. Mix thoroughly, but gently, to combine all the ingredients. (If mixing by hand, combine in a large mixing bowl with a fork; do not pack mixture down.) Heat the oven to 350°F (180°C).

Pack the meat mixture into a 2 quart (2 L) rectangular glass or 9x5x2 inch (23x13x5 cm) ceramic loaf pan, filling mixture right to the corners. Spoon tomato sauce over top, sprinkle with brown sugar, and top with the remaining Parmesan.

Bake the meat loaf in the centre of the oven for 1 1/2 hours. Remove, and let cool for 30 minutes before slicing and serving warm. Or, cool completely, cover and chill overnight. For sandwiches, this terrine may be sliced wafer-thin with ease.

VEAL MARENGO

Here is the classic recipe for any cut of veal, cooked slowly to perfection in a clay baker or casserole with herbs, seasonings and the extra surprise of pimiento-stuffed green olives. Serve it with steamed seasonal vegetables and baked potatoes, and don't forget the sour cream. Serves 5-6.

1 tbsp.	oil	15 mL
3 lbs.	boned veal, any cut	1.5 kg
2	onions, quartered	2
1	clove garlic, peeled and split	1
2	sprigs parsley	2
2 tbsp.	tomato paste	30 mL
1/2 cup	dry white wine	125 mL
	juice of 1/2 lemon	
	salt and pepper to taste	
1/2 lb.	fresh mushrooms	125 g
24	pitted green olives with pimiento	24

Soak the clay baker, top and bottom, for 10 minutes. (Or have ready an ovenproof casserole with lid.) Pat dry and oil the bottom of the baker. Add the veal, onions, garlic and parsley. Mix together the tomato paste and wine. Pour over the meat, along with the lemon juice. Season with salt and pepper or chopped herbs of your choice, such as oregano or marjoram. Cover the dish and put it into a cold oven, then turn the heat to 425°F (220°C) and bake for 1 hour. Remove the dish from the oven and add the mushrooms and olives. Return it to the oven and bake for another 30 minutes, until well-done. Serve immediately.

VEAL ZURICH-STYLE WITH RÖSTI

This is the famed veal dish of Zurich, Switzerland—julienne strips of milk-white veal done up in a fragrant cream sauce with fresh mushrooms. Simple, yet so delicious that seconds are always in order. Serve this dish with a large skillet-sized rösti, *the beloved hash-brown potato pancake of the Swiss—almost the national dish! A lovely, chilled white wine is the perfect beverage. Serves 4.*

1/2 cup	unsalted butter	125 mL
4 tbsp.	minced shallots	60 mL
1/2 lb.	fresh mushrooms, wiped clean	250 g
	and thinly sliced	
1 tbsp.	fresh lemon juice	15 mL
1 1/2 lbs.	tender boneless veal, cut into	750 g
	1 x 1/4 inch (2.5 cm x 6 mm) julienne strips (or	
	substitute turkey breast)	
1/2 cup	dry white wine	125 mL
1 cup	whipping cream	250 mL
	salt and white pepper	
1	*rösti* (shredded potato pancake), 10 inches	1
	(25 cm) wide (recipe follows)	

Melt half the butter in a large, heavy skillet over medium-high heat. Add the shallots and sauté 3-4 minutes, until translucent. Add the mushrooms and sauté 5-6 minutes until just pale golden. Add the lemon juice, increase the heat to high, and reduce all the juices completely, about 3 minutes. Transfer the mushroom mixture to a warm plate, and wipe the skillet dry.

Melt the remaining butter in the skillet over medium-high heat. Pat the veal strips dry, and add them to the skillet, small handfuls at a time. Sauté the veal quickly, 3-4 minutes, to brown very lightly. Lift the veal from the skillet with a slotted spoon and set it aside.

Add the wine to the skillet, and deglaze (draw the juices from the pan) over high heat, stirring until the mixture is glossy and syrupy and reduced by half. Add the cream, and continue to cook the sauce over high heat until it is thickened and bubbly, and reduced slightly. The sauce should be thick enough to coat a spoon.

Add the mushrooms and veal to the sauce, and season to taste with salt and pepper. Cook 2-3 minutes more until heated through. Serve on warmed plates, each portion accompanied by a generous quarter of the potato pancake.

RÖSTI

The traditional *rösti* is made with fresh russet potatoes cooked in their jackets in simmering water until just tender, but still a bit firm. The potatoes are cooled overnight, then peeled, and grated into very long, coarse shreds. This method makes a superb potato pancake.

This version is simplified for the cook with little time on his or her hands. In the freezer case you will find a bag of pre-cooked, pre-shredded hash-brown potato shreds—ready for you to cook. No muss, no fuss.

2 tbsp.	vegetable oil	30 mL
6 tbsp.	butter	90 mL
4 cups	shredded partially-cooked potatoes	1 L
	salt and freshly ground pepper	

Heat the oil and half the butter in a 10-inch (25 cm) non-stick skillet over medium heat. When the butter has foamed and subsided, add the potatoes. Pat down into a flat cake. Brown the pancake, shaking the pan back and forth to loosen the cake, about 8 minutes or until it is a rich golden brown and very crispy. While the pancake is browning, add bits of butter as needed around the edges, allowing the butter to melt and flow underneath.

Place a large, round plate over the skillet. Holding one hand firmly on the plate, flip the skillet over, so that the pancake is on the plate. Melt the remaining butter in the hot skillet, and gently slide the pancake back into the skillet. Brown the other side 5-6 minutes until very crisp, seasoning with salt and pepper. Slide the finished *rösti* onto a warmed plate, cut it into quarters, and serve it with the veal.

ROAST LOIN OF PORK WITH DRIED FRUIT STUFFING

This Scandinavian-inspired recipe for stuffed roast loin of pork is truly delectable. Filled with a savoury-sweet fruit stuffing, the golden brown easy-to-carve roast is finished with a quick pan-sauce of apple jelly and cream. Serve with real mashed potatoes, steamed fresh spinach, chilled lingonberries or cranberry sauce, and hot yeast rolls. Serves 6-8.

1	boneless centre-cut loin of pork, about 5 lbs (2.5 kg), laid out flat	1
4 tbsp.	butter	60 mL
1	small onion, minced	1
1/2 cup	*each* dried apricots, dried pitted prunes, dried apples, all snipped into small dice, rinsed in hot water to plump, and drained	125 mL
3 tbsp.	minced fresh parsley	45 mL
2 tbsp.	fresh lemon juice	30 mL
	grated rind of 1 lemon	
1/2 cup	chopped walnut pieces	125 mL
1 cup	fresh bread crumbs	250 mL
	salt and pepper	
	Apple and Cream Pan-Sauce (recipe follows)	

Bring the pork loin to room temperature, about 1 hour. Meanwhile, heat 2 tbsp. (30 mL) of the butter in a skillet over medium heat until it foams. Add the onion and sauté until softened. Add the snipped dried fruits and parsley, and sauté 4-5 minutes until the fruits are plumped and glossy. Add the lemon juice, rind, and walnut pieces, and sauté 2-3 minutes. Combine the mixture with the bread crumbs, and season to taste with salt and pepper. Set the stuffing aside to cool to room temperature.

Flatten out the boned pork loin, fat side down. Spread the stuffing over the pork, and roll it up tightly. Tie the roast with cotton kitchen string at 2 inch (5 cm) intervals to close.

Heat the remaining 2 tbsp. (30 mL) butter in a roasting pan over medium-high heat. Add the tied roast, and quickly brown on all sides for 6-8 minutes, seasoning with salt and pepper. Meanwhile, heat the oven to 325°F (160°C).

Roast the pork, uncovered, about 2 - 2 1/2 hours, or until it is a rich golden brown. The pork should show no resistance when pierced with a sharp knife tip.

Remove the roast from the oven, and transfer it to a warmed platter. Prepare the Apple and Cream Pan-Sauce. Snip away the strings and discard. Allow the roast to rest 15 minutes before carving for juices to absorb. Carve the meat into 1 inch (2.5 cm) slices, revealing the pretty fruit stuffing in the centre of each slice. Spoon the sauce partially over each slice and serve warm, 2 slices per portion.

APPLE AND CREAM PAN-SAUCE

3/4 cup	dry white wine or dry apple cider	175 mL
1 cup	whipping cream	250 mL
1/3 cup	apple jelly	75 mL
1 tbsp.	Dijon-style or honey mustard	15 mL
	salt and freshly ground black pepper	

Skim the fat from the pan drippings. Heat the drippings and over high heat deglaze (stir up the juices and bits of meat left in the pan) at once with the wine or cider. Cook until the liquid is reduced by half and is thickened and syrupy. Whisk in the cream and cook over high heat until thick and bubbly. The sauce should coat a spoon, and the cream should be reduced by half. Add the apple jelly, and whisk it in until melted. Remove the sauce from the heat, stir in the mustard and season to taste with salt and generous grindings of black pepper. Pour the sauce into a warmed gravy boat, and serve it with the roast pork.

M USTARD SEED COATED CRUSTY ROAST PORK

This savoury mustard-spiked roast pork is pungently crusty on the outside, juicy and tender on the inside. The addition of whole mustard seeds on the crust is a crunchy, eye-appealing addition. Serve with crisp potato pancakes, cool applesauce, fresh butter-glazed carrots and turnips, and creamy scalloped potatoes. Serves 4-6.

1	boneless pork loin roast, 3 1/2 lbs. (1.75 kg), tied	1
1/2 cup	dry sherry or dry apple cider	125 mL
3 tbsp.	*each* cider vinegar and olive oil	45 mL
1	small onion, slivered	1
3	bay leaves, broken in thirds	3
2 tsp.	*each* dried sage and thyme	10 mL
2 tbsp.	soy sauce	30 mL
1 tbsp.	brown sugar	15 mL
3 tbsp.	butter or olive oil	45 mL
	salt and black pepper	
3 tbsp.	*each* honey, Dijon-style mustard and softened butter	45 mL
1/3 cup	bread crumbs	75 mL
1/3 cup	whole mustard seeds	75 mL
1 cup	dry apple cider	250 mL
1/2 cup	cream (optional)	125 mL

Whisk together the sherry (or cider), vinegar, oil, onion, bay leaves, sage, thyme, soy sauce and brown sugar. Pour the marinade over the pork roast, turn to coat, and refrigerate 4-6 hours. Bring the pork to room temperature, lift it from marinade, and pat dry. Discard the marinade.

Heat the oven to 425°F (220°C). Line a shallow roasting pan, just large enough to comfortably hold the roast, with a sheet of baking parchment.

Heat the 3 tbsp. (45 mL) butter or oil (or combination of both) in a skillet over medium-high heat. Quickly brown the pork on all sides, turning. Season liberally with salt and pepper. Place the browned pork in a roasting pan, fat side up. Roast for 10 minutes, reduce the oven temperature to 350°F (180°C) and continue to roast about 1 hour, uncovered, basting with any pan juices that accumulate.

Combine the honey, 3 tbsp. (45 mL) softened butter and crumbs in a small bowl. Remove the roast from the oven, and pack the crumb paste over the top and sides. Sprinkle with the whole mustard seeds, and return the roast to the oven. Continue to roast 30-35 minutes, or until the meat is crusty and golden brown and the seeds are toasted. Do not baste during the final roasting time. Properly roasted pork will show no resistance when pierced with the tip of a sharp knife.

Remove the roasted pork to a warmed platter. Deglaze the pan (stir up any juices and bits of meat clinging to it) over high heat with the 1 cup (250 mL) dry cider. Heat until the liquid is reduced by half, and is thickened and syrupy. Enrich the sauce (if desired) with the cream, heating over high heat until the sauce is bubbly and thick enough to thinly coat a spoon. Season to taste with salt and pepper, if needed.

Carve the roast into 1/2 inch (1 cm) thick slices, allowing several slices per portion. Lightly coat each slice with a spoonful of the sauce. Serve hot or warm.

PORK CHOPS PIZZAIOLA

Anyone who loves pizza (and who doesn't!) will love these spicy chops. Use thick-cut pork loin chops, and braise them with the delicious pizza-like sauce. Serve with pasta on the side, drizzled with a bit of the sauce, and a bright green vegetable. Warm bread is a must to soak up the last bit of sauce. Serves 4.

4	loin pork chops, each cut 1-1 1/4 inch (2.5 - 3 cm) thick	4
2 tbsp.	olive oil	30 mL
	salt and cracked black pepper	
1 cup	chopped onion	250 mL
1	green bell pepper, seeded and de-ribbed, diced	1
2 cups	canned Italian plum tomatoes, coarsely chopped (juices reserved)	500 mL
2	large cloves garlic, minced	2
2 tsp.	*each* sugar and red wine vinegar	10 mL
1 tsp.	*each* dried basil and oregano	5 mL
1/2 cup	sliced pitted black olives	125 mL
2 tbsp.	capers, rinsed	30 mL
4	slices Mozzarella cheese, 1/8 inch (3 mm) thick	4
4 tbsp.	minced fresh parsley	60 mL

Pat the pork chops dry. Heat the olive oil in a skillet just large enough to hold the chops in a single layer. Add the chops, and brown quickly (3-4 minutes per side), seasoning with salt and pepper. Remove the chops to a platter, and set aside.

Add the onion and green pepper to the drippings in the pan. Sauté over medium-high heat 4-5 minutes, until softened and pale golden. Add the tomatoes, garlic, sugar, vinegar, basil and oregano. Cook over high heat 5-6 minutes until most of the liquid is evaporated, and the sauce is thickened. Add the reserved tomato juice, olives, and capers and cook the sauce 5-6 minutes until thickened and pulpy. Taste and correct for salt and pepper.

Add the browned chops to the skillet, mounding sauce on top of each portion. Bring to a simmer, partially cover, and braise over low heat 3/4 - 1 hour, or just until the chops are tender (do not overcook) and the sauce is thick.

Uncover the skillet. Place 1 slice of cheese on top of each chop, cover the skillet, and cook 2-3 minutes, just until the cheese melts. Or run the skillet under the broiler for 1-2 minutes until the cheese is bubbly (make sure the skillet handle is metal and ovenproof).

Serve each chop on a warmed plate, surrounded by the sauce. Sprinkle the cheese-tops with the minced parsley, and serve.

Note: A quick short-cut to this recipe is to follow it exactly, substituting your favourite brand of prepared spaghetti sauce in lieu of preparing your own. Add the olives and capers to the sauce. Use one 12 oz. (375 mL) jar of prepared sauce, the chunkier the better.

The Easy Gourmet features a photograph of this recipe on page 53.

MUSTARD BARBECUED SAUSAGES

Dijon-style mustard, chili sauce and Worcestershire are the secrets of this spicy concoction—guaranteed to please at a Sunday brunch party. Serves 4.

1 lb.	pork, beef, lamb or turkey sausages	500 g
2 tbsp.	olive oil	30 mL
2 tbsp.	tomato or chili sauce	30 mL
2 tsp.	Dijon or other flavourful mustard	10 mL
dash	Worcestershire sauce	dash
drop	hot pepper (Tabasco) sauce	drop
	salt and pepper to taste	

Heat the oven to 400°F (200°C).

Pierce the skin of the sausages with a fork. Place them on a rack on a baking sheet. Mix together the remaining ingredients and spread over the sausages.

Bake for 20 minutes, basting occasionally, until the sausages are well-browned.

Serve hot.

SAVOURY ONION AND LEMON GLAZED PORK CHOPS

This recipe for succulent barbecue-flavoured loin chops is a long-standing family favourite. Skillet-braised with lemon and onion slices, with a pan-sauce of ketchup, brown sugar and spices, these hearty chops make great supper fare. Serve them with broad noodles, fresh broccoli, and a loaf of crisp French bread or a basket of buttermilk biscuits hot from the oven. Serves 4.

4	loin pork chops, cut 1 1/4 inches (3 cm) thick	4
2 tbsp.	vegetable oil	30 mL
1	large onion, peeled and sliced into eight rounds, 1/4 inch (6 mm) thick	1
1	large lemon, including rind, sliced into 1/8 inch (3 mm) rounds	1
1 tbsp.	Worcestershire sauce	15 mL
	salt and black pepper	
1/2 cup	tomato ketchup	125 mL
4 tbsp.	brown sugar, packed	60 mL
4 dashes	ground cinnamon	4 dashes
4 dashes	ground allspice	4 dashes
1/3 cup	water, beer or sherry	75 mL

Over medium-high heat, heat the oil in a heavy skillet large enough to hold the chops in a single layer. Add the pork chops and brown them quickly on both sides, 2-3 minutes.

Drain the fat from the skillet and discard. Season the chops with salt and pepper on both sides. Sprinkle Worcestershire on the tops. On each chop lay 2 rounds of onion, slightly overlapping, and 2 slices of lemon, slightly overlapping. Spoon the ketchup over the chops. Top each chop with 1 tbsp. (15 mL) brown sugar, and sprinkle lightly with cinnamon and allspice.

Carefully pour the water (or beer or sherry) into the bottom of the skillet without disturbing the assembled chops. Bring the liquid to a simmer, partially cover the skillet, and cook the chops over medium-low heat about 1 1/2 hours or until tender. Using a bulb-baster, baste the chops with pan sauce every 15 minutes, allowing the sauce to flow gently over each portion.

The finished pork chops should be tender when pierced, the onion and lemon should be translucent and golden and the sauce should be syrupy and thickened.

Remove the chops from the skillet with a spatula, taking care to keep the onion and lemon on top. Place on heated plates. Increase the heat under the skillet to high, and reduce the sauce (if needed), stirring, until it is glossy and syrupy. Nap each portion of meat with several spoonfuls of sauce, and serve at once.

COUNTRY HAM-STEAKS WITH "RED-EYE GRAVY"

Good North American "country" cooks like to slice up thick slices of ham to cook up a real breakfast! Nothing is more inviting than succulent pan-fried ham slices with this pungent "red-eye" gravy, served up with a couple of sunnyside-up eggs, and a batch of hot biscuits—all washed down with strong, hot coffee to get the weekend morning going. Serves 4.

4	generous slices pre-cooked baked ham, cut 1/2 inch (1 cm) thick, or round ham steaks, bone-in	4
2-3	small pieces ham fat	2-3
1 tbsp.	brown sugar	15 mL
1 cup	strong black coffee	250 mL

Heat a large cast-iron skillet over medium heat. Trim 2-3 small pieces of white fat from the ham, and fry until crisped. Remove the fat pieces, and discard.

Fry the ham steaks in the hot skillet, several minutes per side, until lightly coloured and sizzling hot. Remove the steaks to a warmed platter. Stir in the sugar, and caramelize 2 minutes.

Pour the coffee into the hot skillet, increase the heat to high, and boil briskly, scraping in the brown bits that cling to the bottom of the skillet, until the sauce is thickened, syrupy, glossy—and bright red! Pour the sauce over the ham steaks, and serve at once.

HAM AND MUSHROOM RING AROUND

A creamy blend of ham and mushrooms, surrounded by a crispy, golden puff of freshly-baked Yorkshire Pudding... add a crunchy green salad and you have a heavenly luncheon or light supper! Serves 2.

Prepare Yorkshire Pudding batter (page 24) and set it aside.

Next prepare the filling:

2 tbsp.	butter	30 mL
1	small onion, chopped	1
1	large mushroom, sliced	1
1 tbsp.	all-purpose flour	15 mL
1/2 cup	chicken stock	125 mL
4 oz.	Black Forest ham, chopped	125 g
1	tomato, seeded and quartered	1
1 tbsp.	grated Parmesan cheese	15 mL
	chopped fresh parsley for garnish	

Heat the oven to 450°F (230°C). Generously grease or butter an 8 inch (20 cm) cake tin with 2 inch (5 cm) sides.

Melt the butter in a medium skillet. Add the onion and sauté for a few minutes, then add the mushroom. Cook briefly. Take the pan off the heat and whisk in the flour and the stock. Return to medium heat and simmer for about 5 minutes. Remove from the heat and add the ham and tomato.

Place the greased pan in the oven to heat, about 3 minutes. Into the hot pan, pour the Yorkshire Pudding batter. Spoon the prepared ham mixture into the centre of the batter, leaving a border of about 2 inches (5 cm).

Return to the hot oven and bake until well puffed and very dark golden brown. Serve immediately.

AM WITH CURRIED FRUIT

Ham with fruit and curry butter gives an unusual blend of flavours that will bring them back for seconds any time of the year. Ready in an hour, it is set off perfectly with steamed rice, a crunchy salad of raw vegetables and a basket of whole wheat buns. Serves 4.

4	slices ham, 1/2 inch (1 cm) thick	4
1	14 oz. (398 mL) can pineapple tidbits	1
1	14 oz. (398 mL) can pear halves	1
1	14 oz. (398 mL) can peach halves	1
12	maraschino cherries	12
3/4 cup	brown sugar, packed	175 mL
4 tbsp.	melted butter	60 mL
4 tsp.	curry powder	20 mL

Heat the oven to 350°F (180°C). Trim excess fat from the ham slices and place them in a greased baking dish large enough to hold them in a single layer.

Drain the pineapple, pears and peaches into a bowl and measure out 2/3 cup (150 mL) of the combined juices. Pour the juices over the ham. Bake the ham 30 minutes, basting frequently with the juices. Remove the baking dish from the oven and spoon all of the drained fruit over top. Sprinkle cherries over all.

Combine the sugar, butter and curry powder and drop the mixture by spoonfuls on top of the fruit. Return the dish to the oven and bake for a further 20 minutes, basting frequently. To serve, place a piece of ham on each plate with a spoonful of rice to the side. Top all with the fruit and juices.

FAMILY FAVOURITE CIDER-GLAZED COUNTRY HAM

This special ham is festive enough for the holiday table—always anticipated, always savoured with gusto! A slow simmer in cider and water results in a succulent, juicy, tender ham. The mustardy-brown sugar glaze insures a rich golden brown crust. Simple to prepare, this ham almost takes care of itself... with raves and calls for seconds guaranteed. Serves 12-16.

1	18-20 lb. (8-9 kg) whole smoked ham, fully cooked with bone in and rind on	1
2 quarts	apple cider	2 L
1/2 cup	whole cloves	125 mL
1 cup	brown sugar, packed	250 mL
1/3 cup	maple syrup, honey or molasses	75 mL
1/2 cup	grainy mustard	125 mL
1/4 tsp.	*each* ground allspice and cinnamon	1 mL
2 tbsp.	cider or sherry	30 mL

Rinse ham and rind with cool water. Place it in a very large stock pot or deep roasting pan, pour in the cider, and add water to cover. Bring the liquid to a gentle simmer, partially cover the pot, and cook gently 2-3 hours (this will tenderize the ham and draw out the saltiness).

Turn off the heat, and allow the ham to cool in the liquid until it is barely warm. Remove the ham from the liquid. Carefully peel away the heavy rind and discard. Leave the remaining white fat 1/2 inch (1 cm) thick, and score into it a decorative "diamond" pattern with a sharp knife. Stud the centre of each diamond with a whole clove. Place the ham in an open roaster lined with baking parchment or ovenproof brown paper. Heat the oven to 325°F (160°C).

Prepare the glaze by combining the brown sugar, maple syrup (or honey or molasses), mustard, spices and cider (or sherry). Brush the glaze generously over the top and sides of the prepared ham. Roast the ham, uncovered, 1 - 1 1/2 hours, or until it is golden brown and heated through. Basting is unnecessary. Remove the ham from the oven and allow it to rest 20 minutes before carving to allow the juices to be re-absorbed. Place the ham on a large warmed platter, and garnish as desired. Serve in thick or thin vertical slices, allowing a bit of the glazed crust to surround each slice.

Opposite: (Top to bottom) Pork Chops Pizzaiola (page 46); Italian Sausages with "Tri-Colore" Peppers (page 37).

DEVILED COUNTRY-STYLE PORK RIBS

Thick, meaty "country-style" pork ribs are delicious with this mustard-spiked deviled crusting. Beef short ribs may also be used in this recipe, for a change of pace. Either way, serve the ribs with old-fashioned scalloped potatoes, fresh spinach or broccoli, and hot biscuits. Serves 4-6.

1	small onion, minced	1
1/3 cup	cider vinegar	75 mL
1/3 cup	vegetable oil	75 mL
2 tbsp.	brown sugar	30 mL
4 tbsp.	*each* Dijon-style mustard and grainy mustard	60 mL
1/3 cup	finely minced fresh parsley	75 mL
2 tsp.	*each* salt and black pepper	10 mL
1/2 tsp.	cayenne pepper	2 mL
3 lbs.	meaty country-style pork ribs	1.5 kg

Combine the onion, vinegar, oil, sugar, mustards, parsley, salt, pepper and cayenne. Whisk until smooth. Pour the mixture over the pork ribs, turn to coat, and marinate 3-4 hours or overnight, covered. Heat the oven to 400°F (200°C).

Lift the ribs from the marinade, shaking off the excess. Place them on a lightly oiled rack set in a shallow roasting pan, fat side up. Roast the ribs in the centre of the oven 20 minutes, reduce the heat to 350°F (180°C), and continue roasting about 1 1/4 hours or until the meat is a rich golden brown and tender.

Serve the ribs on a warm platter, hot from the oven.

APRICOT AND ORANGE GLAZED "STICKY" BABY BACK RIBS

Serve these "have-to-be-tasted-to-be-believed" baby back ribs in hearty portions, one full slab per person as a full meal, or half-slabs as appetizers. Accompany with crusty corn bread, a fresh tomato and onion salad, and seasonal corn-on-the-cob slathered with butter. Serves 4-8.

4	pork baby back ribs (whole slabs) (4-5 lbs. (2-2 1/2 kg)), trimmed lengthwise to 3 inches (7.5 cm)	4
2	oranges, halved	2
	salt and black pepper to taste	
1/3 cup	*each* fresh orange juice and cider vinegar, mixed together	75 mL
3 cups	Apricot and Orange Glaze (recipe follows)	750 mL

Prepare the Apricot and Orange Glaze.

Rub both sides of the ribs with the cut oranges, and allow to sit at room temperature on a shallow baking sheet for 30 minutes. Heat the oven to 350°F (180°C).

Place the ribs on the roasting rack, and brush with the combined orange juice and vinegar. Season liberally with salt and pepper on both sides. Place the ribs in the oven, top side up, and roast 35 minutes, or until light golden brown in colour.

Brush the ribs liberally with the prepared glaze. Return the ribs to the oven, and roast an additional 30-40 minutes, or until the ribs are a rich, deep golden brown, slightly charred at the edges, and the meat has pulled away slightly from the tips of the bones. Baste the ribs with the glaze several times during roasting.

Remove the ribs from the oven, and transfer to a carving board or platter. Allow the ribs to "rest" for 10 minutes before serving.

Serve one full slab per portion for a full meal, half-slabs for appetizer portions. Pass sharp steak knives to cut down through the meaty, tender ribs. Offer any remaining glaze for dipping.

APRICOT AND ORANGE GLAZE

Makes about 3 cups (750 mL).

3 tbsp.	vegetable oil	45 mL
1	medium-sized onion, minced	1
2	large cloves garlic, minced	2
4 tbsp.	cider vinegar	60 mL
4 tbsp.	fresh orange juice	60 mL
1	16 oz. (375 mL) jar apricot preserves (about 1 1/2 cups (375 mL))	1
1 tbsp.	*each* finely grated orange rind, soy sauce and Worcestershire sauce	15 mL
3 tbsp.	brown sugar, packed	45 mL
pinch	*each* ground cloves and ground cinnamon	pinch
10 drops	liquid hot pepper (Tabasco) sauce	10 drops
3 tbsp.	butter	45 mL

Heat the oil in a deep saucepan over medium heat. Add the onion and sauté 6 minutes. Stir in the garlic, and sauté 3-4 minutes. Add the vinegar and orange juice, and simmer the mixture 3-4 minutes until bubbly.

Add the apricot preserves, orange rind, soy sauce, Worcestershire, brown sugar, cloves, cinnamon and Tabasco. Bring the mixture to a simmer and cook 30 minutes, until the flavours are blended and the sauce is thickened. Finally, stir in the butter, and cook until melted and bubbly.

The Easy Gourmet features a photograph of this recipe on the front cover.

PORK MEDALLIONS WITH APRICOT SOUR CREAM SAUCE

M

The humble pork chop goes uptown in this elegant entrée. Just add fluffy rice mixed with toasted almonds, and a bright green vegetable, and you've turned a dinner into an event. Serves 4.

1/4 lb.	dried apricots	125 g
2 tbsp.	sherry or apple juice	30 mL
	juice of 1/2 lemon	
1/2 tsp.	salt	2 mL
1/4 tsp.	pepper	1 mL
4	boneless pork loin chops, cut about 1 inch (2.5 cm) thick	4
2 tbsp.	brandy	30 mL
1/2 cup	sour cream	125 mL
	chopped parsley for garnish	

Place the apricots and sherry (or apple juice) in a small microproof dish. Cover the fruit with water and microwave on HIGH 100% power 3 minutes to plump. Cool slightly, drain off the juice and reserve. Stir the lemon juice, salt and pepper into the reserved juice. Trim the fat from the pork chops and shape into medallions, securing with toothpicks.

Heat a browning skillet. Add butter and immediately add the pork medallions, pressing each piece firmly onto the surface of the skillet to get the maximum browning effect. Return skillet to the microwave and cook on MEDIUM 50% power 4-5 minutes. Turn the pork over and microwave on MEDIUM 50% power for a further 4-5 minutes.

Drain any excess fat from the skillet. Add the drained apricots to the pork. Place the brandy in a 1-cup (250 mL) microproof measure. Microwave on HIGH 100% power 20-25 seconds. Ignite the brandy and pour over pork. Microwave on MEDIUM 50% power 10 minutes, turning the pork over halfway through the cooking time. Remove the pork from the skillet, remove toothpicks, cover with foil and let stand.

Combine the reserved apricot juice and the sour cream in the skillet. Microwave on MEDIUM 50% power 2-4 minutes until heated through, stirring once during the cooking time. Pour sauce over the pork, garnish with parsley and serve.

GARLIC AND HERBED ROAST LEG OF LAMB

This method of roasting a leg of lamb gives superb results. Whenever you can obtain fresh local lamb, grab up a leg and treat your family or friends to this version. Flavoured with a buttery rub of fresh mint, rosemary and garlic, and roasted on a bed of sliced lemons, the lamb turns out tender and tasty, with fragrant and savoury pan juices. Serve with fresh green beans, tiny red-skinned nugget potatoes, and a warm baguette. Serves 6.

1	leg of lamb (bone in), 5-6 lbs. (2.5-3 kg)	1
2	lemons, thinly sliced, rind and all	2
6 tbsp.	butter, softened	90 mL
2	large cloves garlic, minced	2
4 tbsp.	finely minced fresh mint	60 mL
2 tbsp.	finely minced fresh rosemary	30 mL
2 tsp.	*each* coarse salt and cracked black pepper	10 mL

Bring the lamb to room temperature. Heat the oven to 325°F (160°C). Line a roasting pan with the slices of lemon, just large enough for a "bed" for the leg of lamb.

In a small bowl, combine the butter, garlic, mint, rosemary, salt and pepper to form a paste. Rub the flavoured butter all over the outside of the lamb.

Place the lamb on the bed of lemons. Roast about 2 - 2 1/4 hours for rare, 140°F (60°C) on the meat thermometer; a few minutes longer for medium rare, 160°F (70°C) on the meat thermometer. The outside should be crusty and a rich golden brown, the inside juicy and succulent, and a rosy pink. Baste the lamb every 20 minutes during roasting with the collected pan juices.

Remove the lamb from the oven. Allow it to stand 15-20 minutes before carving horizontally (with the grain, French-style) in thick or thin slices. Serve the slices napped with the warm pan juices.

The Easy Gourmet features a photograph of this recipe on page 35.

L EG OF LAMB SPICED INDIAN STYLE

The authentic taste of India permeates this succulent roast lamb dish. The meat is marinated overnight in an intriguing blend of spices and yogourt, then roasted until crisp and golden. It may seem that you have a lot of marinade, but it all blends into the lamb as it cooks. Serve with Indian accompaniments such as rice, spiced vegetables and chutney, or as a more traditional meal with roast potatoes, broccoli and carrots. Serves 4.

1	3 1/2 - 4 lb. (1.75 - 2 kg) leg of lamb	1
1 1/2 cups	plain yogourt	375 mL
2	large onions, peeled and chopped very fine or grated	2
4	cloves garlic, crushed	4
1	1 inch (2.5 cm) piece fresh ginger, peeled and grated	1
2 tbsp.	ground almonds	30 mL
2 tsp.	*each* ground coriander, turmeric, chili and curry powder	10 mL
1 tsp.	*each* ground cumin, paprika and whole mustard seeds	5 mL
	juice of 1 lime or lemon	
2 tbsp.	tomato paste	30 mL
4	whole cloves	4

Trim the lamb, removing any skin or fat. Place the meat in a large dish. In a medium bowl, combine the yogourt with the onion, garlic, ginger, almonds, coriander, turmeric, chili, curry, cumin, paprika, mustard seeds, lime juice and tomato paste. Mix well. Stick the cloves into the meat. Thoroughly cover the meat with yogourt mixture and prick it all over with a fork. Cover it with plastic wrap and marinate in the refrigerator overnight.

Heat the oven to 375°F (190°C). Place the meat and marinade in a foil-lined roasting pan and roast, loosely covered with foil, for 1 1/2 hours. Remove the cover and roast a further 1 - 1 1/2 hours until the meat is cooked and the outside is crusty and golden. Baste occasionally with the marinade. Let it rest for a few minutes, then slice and serve.

 # LAMB WITH MUSTARD SEED COATING

Tender, juicy, always satisfying, lamb is becoming more and more popular. The unusual crunchy coating called for in this recipe sets off the flavour of the lamb perfectly. One little secret of success for this dish: have the meat at room temperature before it is cooked—a few minutes on the DEFROST setting of the microwave will make all the difference. Simple oven-browned potatoes and tiny green peas round out this special dinner. Serves 6.

2	racks of lamb, approx. 1 1/2 lbs. (750 g) each	2
1	clove garlic, crushed	1
3 tbsp.	mustard seeds, crushed	45 mL
1 tsp.	ground ginger	5 mL
1 tsp.	ground black pepper	5 mL
1 tsp.	salt	5 mL

Remove the skin from the lamb and cut off any excess fat. Score diagonal cuts through the fat on each rack about 1 inch (2.5 cm) apart. Rub the crushed garlic into the fat.

Mix the remaining ingredients together and press the mixture over the fat side of the lamb.

Place the racks fat side up on a microwave roasting rack, placing the thicker parts towards the outside edge of the rack. Microwave on MEDIUM HIGH 70% power, allowing 9-11 minutes per pound for a medium degree of doneness, 11-13 minutes per pound for well done.

Remove the lamb from the roasting rack onto a platter, cover with two layers of foil and let stand for about 10 minutes.

To serve, slice the lamb between the rib bones.

SPICY LAMB PASTITSIO

This wonderful ground lamb and pasta dish from Greece makes great family or company fare. The lovely baked creamy topping contrasts with the hearty meat layer and buttery pasta layer. Serve it with a Greek salad full of fresh cucumbers, tomatoes, slivered onions and olives, and pass a basketful of warm pita or sesame-topped bread. Serves 6-8.

The Meat Sauce:

1 tbsp.	olive oil	15 mL
1	small onion, minced	1
1	large clove garlic, minced	1
1 lb.	lean ground lamb	500 g
1 tsp.	*each* salt and pepper	5 mL
1/3 cup	dried currants, rinsed and drained	75 mL
1/2 cup	dry red wine	125 mL
1/4 tsp.	*each* ground cinnamon and nutmeg	2 mL
1 tsp.	dried oregano, crumbled	5 mL
1 cup	tomato sauce	250 mL
1/3 cup	minced fresh parsley	75 mL

Heat the olive oil in a deep saucepan over medium-high heat. Add the onion and garlic and sauté 5-7 minutes until softened. Add the lamb, and brown it with the onions until no pink colour remains. Add the salt, pepper, rinsed currants, wine, cinnamon, nutmeg and oregano. Heat until bubbly and cook 10 minutes. Add the tomato sauce and parsley, partially cover the sauce, and cook 25 minutes. Set aside.

This sauce may be prepared up to 3 days ahead of time, and kept covered in the refrigerator. Bring it to room temperature before assembling the dish.

The Pasta:

1 lb.	long macaroni (penne or ziti)	500 g
4 tbsp.	butter	60 mL
1/2 cup	finely grated Parmesan cheese	125 mL
1/4 tsp.	ground nutmeg	1 mL
	salt and pepper	
2	eggs, beaten	2

Cook the pasta *al dente* (slightly firm to the bite) in boiling water with 1 tbsp. (15 mL) each salt and olive oil added. Drain. Melt the butter until it is a nutty, golden brown, and pour sizzling hot over the drained warm pasta. Toss to coat, add the Parmesan, and season with the nutmeg, salt and pepper. Cool to room temperature, then combine with the beaten eggs. Set aside.

The Custard Topping:

1/3 cup	butter	75 mL
1/3 cup	all-purpose flour	75 mL
3 cups	milk	750 mL
1/4 tsp.	*each* salt, pepper and nutmeg	1 mL
2/3 cup	freshly grated Parmesan cheese	150 mL

Heat the butter in a deep saucepan over medium heat. When it foams, whisk in the flour, and cook 3 minutes. Add the milk, whisking constantly, just until the milk comes to a boil and the sauce thickens, 4-5 minutes. Remove the sauce from the heat, and season with salt, pepper and nutmeg. Set aside.

To assemble the Pastitsio, lightly oil the bottom and sides of a 9 x 13x 3 inch (23 x 32 x 7.5 cm) ovenproof baking dish. Cover the bottom ofthe dish with half the pasta, top with the meat sauce, and cover withthe remainder of the pasta. Make sure the top is level. Cover with the custard sauce, and dust the top with the Parmesan. You may stop at this point and refrigerate the dish for several hours, uncovered.

Heat the oven to 350°F (180°C). Bake the Pastitsio for 50-60 minutes, or until the top is golden brown and puffy. Cool the dish for 15 minutes before serving.

SPICED PINE-NUT LAMB BURGERS

These spicy, succulent lamb burgers are a snap to prepare, and provide a wonderful, unusual dinner with a Middle Eastern flavour. Serve them with a fluffy rice pilaf, fresh green beans, an eggplant and zucchini ratatouille, and a warm loaf of sesame-topped French bread or warm pita breads. Serves 4-6.

2 tbsp.	unsalted butter	30 mL
1 cup	minced onion	250 mL
1/3 cup	minced fresh parsley	75 mL
1/3 cup	pine nuts	75 mL
4 tbsp.	dried currants, rinsed in warm water	60 mL
1 tbsp.	minced dried mint leaves	15 mL
1 tsp.	*each* salt, pepper and ground cumin	5 mL
2 lbs.	lean ground lamb	1 kg

Heat the butter in a skillet over medium-high heat, add the onion and sauté until softened and pale golden, about 5 minutes. Add the parsley, pine nuts, and currants and sauté 4-5 minutes until the nuts are golden and the currants are plump. Add the mint, salt, pepper and cumin, and heat through 1 minute. Set the mixture aside to cool to room temperature.

Gently combine the lamb with the cooled mixture, combining thoroughly and kneading 2-3 minutes. With moistened hands, form the mixture into 4-6 thick oval patties. Cover loosely, and chill the patties 1-2 hours to firm.

Broil or pan-fry the burgers until they are crusty brown on the outside, and juicy and a bit pink on the inside, about 4-5 minutes per side. Serve the burgers hot.

POULTRY

Poultry, just about everyone's favourite light and luscious meat, fills the "bill of fare" on many occasions—a simple supper for two or a feast for friends. At Safeway, you'll find fresh and frozen poultry for everything from Indonesian Chicken Saté to Turkey Enchiladas; and specialty birds—duck and Cornish game hen—are basic stock.

CRISPY CRUNCHY CHICKEN

Prepared with the simplest ingredients and topped with a golden coating of corn chip or potato chip crumbs, this one is a favourite with the younger set. It is tasty hot or cold, and perfect alongside baked potatoes, fresh green vegetables and a dish of hot salsa. Serves 4-6.

	grated peel and juice of 1 lemon	
1	clove garlic, crushed	1
3 tbsp.	butter, melted	45 mL
1 cup	finely crushed corn chips, potato chips, corn flakes or crackers	250 mL
1/2 tsp.	pure chili powder or to taste	2 mL
2 lbs.	chicken pieces	1 kg
	lemon wedges and parsley for garnish	

Heat the oven to 400°F (200°C). In a shallow dish combine the lemon peel, juice, garlic and butter. In a second dish combine the chips and chili powder. Dip the chicken pieces in the butter mixture, then coat with the crushed chip mixture. Arrange the chicken on a foil-lined baking sheet with sides. Loosely cover with foil.

Bake for 40 minutes. Remove the foil and bake, uncovered, about 20 minutes longer or until golden and tender.

Garnish with fresh lemon wedges and parsley, and serve at once.

BEST EVER "OLD-FASHIONED" FRIED CHICKEN

This is a delicious method of preparing your own fried chicken—crispy and crunchy on the outside, juicy and tender on the inside, the kind of chicken that will have them begging for seconds. The special technique of coating the chicken and "air drying" it for 2 hours insures a tasty crust that stays on. Serve it with old-fashioned mashed potatoes, creamed corn, broiled tomatoes, steamed green peas, and a basket of hot biscuits. Serves 4.

1	frying chicken, cut up, about 3 1/2 lbs. (1.75 kg)	1
1 cup	buttermilk	250 mL
1 1/2 cups	all-purpose flour	375 mL
1 tsp.	*each* salt, black pepper, paprika, sage, thyme and garlic salt	5 mL
	vegetable oil or peanut oil (peanut oil gives a wonderful result) for frying	
	Farm-Style Cream Gravy (optional) (recipe follows)	

Rinse the chicken with cool water, and pat it completely dry. Soak the chicken in the buttermilk for 1 hour, turning to coat. Combine the flour, salt, pepper, paprika, sage, thyme and garlic salt by shaking them together in a brown paper bag. Remove the chicken pieces from the buttermilk, and shake off the excess.

Shake the chicken pieces, two at a time, in the seasoned flour mixture, coating each piece evenly. Place the coated chicken on a wire rack, and allow it to "air dry" 2 hours at room temperature.

Heat the oil in a large, heavy 12-14 inch (30-35 cm) skillet to a depth of 1 1/2 inches (3.5 cm) over medium-high heat. To test the frying temperature, drop a pinch of flour into the hot oil—the flour will float to the top at once and "sizzle" when the oil is ready for frying.

The Easy Gourmet features a photograph of this recipe on page 71.

Place the chicken pieces in the pan, skin side down, in a single layer without crowding (leave spaces between the pieces so that the chicken can crisp evenly). Cook the chicken about 12-15 minutes until golden brown. Using tongs, carefully turn each piece, taking care not to pierce the skin or flesh. Brown the chicken an additional 18-20 minutes, or until the juices run clear when the chicken is pierced near the bone with a sharp knife.

Lift the chicken pieces out and drain them on brown paper. Serve hot, warm or cool. If you are preparing the gravy, serve it with hot or warm chicken only.

FARM-STYLE CREAM GRAVY

6 tbsp.	pan drippings, including the browned bits in the bottom of the skillet	90 mL
1/3 cup	all-purpose flour	75 mL
1	small clove garlic, minced (optional)	1
1 tbsp.	fresh lemon juice	15 mL
2 1/2 cups	milk or half-and-half cream	625 mL
	salt	
	cracked black pepper	

Remove all but 6 tbsp. (90 mL) of the drippings from the skillet. Blend the flour into the reserved drippings in the pan, stirring with a wooden spoon to loosen the browned bits. Cook the flour and drippings over medium heat, stirring constantly, until bubbly and pale golden in colour, about 5 minutes. Add the garlic and fry 1 minute. Add the lemon juice, and cook 1 minute more. Slowly whisk in the milk, and continue to cook the gravy until it thickens enough to coat a spoon. Season to taste with salt and a generous amount of pepper. Whisk smooth, and serve in a warmed gravy boat. A bit of this gravy is divine spooned over split biscuits!

VEN-FRIED HERBED CHICKEN

This quick and easy oven-fried chicken is sure to become a family favourite. Prepare the full recipe—it is great hot from the oven, and just as good served cold as picnic fare. Accompany it with potato salad, hot dinner rolls with butter, and a sliced tomato salad. Serves 6-8.

3	whole chicken breasts, halved	3
6	chicken leg-thigh pieces	6
1 cup	all-purpose flour	250 mL
1 tbsp.	*each* salt, black pepper and paprika	15 mL
2	eggs, lightly beaten	2
1/2 cup	milk or buttermilk	125 mL
1 1/2 cups	bread crumbs	375 mL
3/4 cup	grated Parmesan cheese	175 mL
1 tbsp.	*each* dried oregano, thyme and basil, finely crumbled	15 mL
	oil	

Rinse the chicken pieces in cool water, and pat them dry. Combine the flour, salt, pepper and paprika in a brown paper bag. Shake the chicken pieces in the flour, coating lightly and shaking off the excess.

Beat the eggs and milk (or buttermilk, for a tangier taste) together in a shallow bowl. In another bowl, combine the crumbs, Parmesan, oregano, thyme and basil. Dip the flour-dusted chicken pieces in the egg-wash, and then carefully in the crumb mixture to coat evenly. Place the chicken on a wire rack to "air dry" in a cool kitchen for 1 hour (this will "set" the coating).

Lightly oil a baking sheet with 1 inch (2.5 cm) sides (or line a baking sheet with baking parchment, lightly oiled, to insure a quick clean-up). Place the chicken pieces on the baking sheet, top sides up. Heat the oven to 350°F (180°C).

Bake the chicken on the centre rack until the meat is tender and the crust is crispy and golden brown, about 45 minutes. Remove the chicken from the oven, let it cool 15 minutes, and serve, or chill it and serve it later.

CHICKEN CORDON BLEU

This classic recipe with its blend of rich flavours adapts very well to the microwave, turning out moist and tender every time. You can even make it ahead, for an elegant busy-day dinner. Try topping it with creamy Hollandaise, and serve with tender-crisp steamed vegetables. Serves 6.

3	whole boneless chicken breasts, halved	3
6	thin slices prosciutto	6
3	thin slices Swiss cheese	3
1	egg, beaten	1
1 tbsp.	milk	15 mL
1 cup	seasoned dry bread crumbs	250 mL

Carefully flatten each chicken breast half with a meat mallet.

Place breasts skinned side down. On top of each, arrange one slice each of prosciutto and half a slice of Swiss cheese, tucking in the edges of the prosciutto and cheese to fit.

Fold the chicken in half over the ham and cheese. Seal the edges firmly with a meat mallet. The chicken may be covered with plastic wrap and refrigerated at this point.

Before cooking, mix together the egg and milk. Then coat each sealed chicken breast with the egg-wash, and thoroughly cover each piece with seasoned bread crumbs.

Arrange the chicken "bicycle spoke" fashion on a round microproof platter, with the thicker edges of the chicken towards the outside of the dish.

Microwave on MEDIUM HIGH 70% power 6-7 minutes. Rearrange and turn pieces over. Microwave on MEDIUM HIGH 70% power for a further 6-7 minutes.

Let stand, uncovered, for about 5 minutes before serving.

CLASSIC ITALIAN CHICKEN

The best loved flavours of Italy blend together in this fragrant, satisfying dinner. Serve the chicken over hot spaghetti with tangy Parmesan cheese, and complement it with steamed zucchini and big crusty Italian rolls—buon appetito! Serves 4.

2 tbsp.	oil	30 mL
2 tbsp.	butter	30 mL
2 lbs.	chicken pieces	1 kg
1	medium onion, coarsely chopped	1
1	clove garlic, crushed	1
1	14 oz. (398 mL) can tomatoes, drained	1
1	7 1/2 oz. (213 mL) can tomato sauce	1
2 tbsp.	chopped fresh parsley	30 mL
1 tbsp.	chopped fresh basil *or*	15 mL
1 tsp.	dried basil	5 mL
	salt and pepper to taste	

Heat the oil and butter in a large skillet and brown the chicken on both sides. Remove it from the pan onto a warm plate. In the same skillet, fry the onion over medium heat until tender. Add the garlic and cook for 1 minute. Return the chicken to the pan along with any juices that may have accumulated. Stir in the remaining ingredients. Cover with a lid or foil and reduce the heat. Cook slowly until tender, about 1 1/2 hours. Stir occasionally and add water as necessary to prevent the dish from drying out or burning.

Serve at once on warmed plates.

Opposite: Best Ever "Old-Fashioned" Fried Chicken (page 66).

CHICKEN STACKS WITH BACON AND CHEESES

A layered dish that is beautiful to look at and even better to eat, this is a simple dinner for two that can be prepared ahead. Serve it with pan-fried potatoes and steamed buttered broccoli. Serves 2.

1	whole boneless chicken breast, skinned and halved	1
2 tbsp.	flour	30 mL
1/4 tsp.	salt	1 mL
pinch	pepper	pinch
1 tbsp.	butter or margarine	15 mL
1/2 tbsp.	vegetable oil	7 mL
1	clove garlic, crushed	1
4	tomato slices	4
4	thin slices Swiss cheese	4
4	strips bacon, cooked until crisp, halved	4
1 tbsp.	grated Parmesan cheese	15 mL
2 tbsp.	chicken bouillon, stock or apple juice	30 mL
	chopped parsley for garnish	

Heat the oven to 350°F (180°C). Slice each chicken breast half in half again. Place each piece between two sheets of waxed paper and beat with a wooden mallet or rolling pin until half the original thickness. Mix the flour, salt and pepper on a large plate. Dip the chicken in the flour to coat, shaking off any excess.

In a large skillet, melt the butter with the oil. Over medium heat, sauté the garlic for 30 seconds. Place the chicken in the skillet and sauté about 2 1/2 minutes on each side, or until lightly browned.

Place the chicken in a shallow buttered 7 inch (18 cm) diameter ovenproof dish in a single layer. Arrange a slice of tomato on each piece of chicken, then a slice of Swiss cheese big enough to almost cover the chicken. Lay two pieces of bacon on each chicken piece, sprinkle with Parmesan and pour the chicken bouillon over all. (The dish may be made ahead to this point, then covered and refrigerated. Allow a little longer for heating through.)

Bake, covered, until the chicken is heated through and the cheese is melted, about 15 minutes. Sprinkle with parsley.

L EMON-HERB CHICKEN WITH VEGETABLES

This easiest of all chicken recipes is a favourite—broiled crispy and slightly charred on the ouside, juicy and moist on the inside, with accompanying fresh vegetables broiled right along with the chicken. Serve this chicken warm, not hot, to allow time for some of the herb-flavoured juices to soak into the tender meat. Pass around lots of warm crusty bread. Serves 4.

1	plump frying chicken, quartered, about 3-3 1/2 lbs. (1.5-1.75 kg)	1
6 tbsp.	olive oil	90 mL
1/3 cup	fresh lemon juice	75 mL
1 tsp.	*each* salt and black pepper	5 mL
2 tsp.	*each* dried tarragon, oregano and thyme	10 mL
4	zucchini, washed, dried and split in half lengthwise	4
4	yellow crook-neck squash, washed, dried and split in half lengthwise	4

Rinse the chicken with cool water, and pat completely dry. Line a broiler pan with aluminum foil. Brush the chicken quarters with the combined olive oil, lemon juice, salt, pepper, tarragon, oregano and thyme. Marinate at room temperature for 30 minutes. Heat the broiler.

Place the chicken skin side down on the lined pan, reserving the marinade. Surround with the halved squashes, cut side up. Brush the squash halves with marinade.

Broil the chicken and vegetables 6-8 inches (15-20 cm) from the heat source for 15 minutes, brushing once or twice with reserved marinade. Turn the chicken and continue to broil, basting with pan juices several times until the chicken is tender, the juices just run clear when the meat is pierced with a knife tip, and the skin is a rich golden brown and slightly charred, about 15-18 minutes more. Remove the squash halves as soon as they are golden brown and bubbly on top, and crisp-tender inside. Enjoy!

UNGARIAN PAPRIKA CHICKEN

Try this ideal family supper—tender chicken cooked in a mildly spiced tomato sauce and topped with sour cream. Toss a salad and cook some rice to go with it while the chicken simmers in the oven. Serves 4.

4	chicken pieces (leg, breast or thigh) cut into serving-size portions	4
4 tbsp.	all-purpose flour	60 mL
1/2 tsp.	salt	2 mL
3 tbsp.	margarine or butter	45 mL
1	medium onion, chopped	1
2/3 cup	tomato juice	150 mL
1 cup	chicken stock or broth	250 mL
2 tbsp.	paprika	30 mL
1 tsp.	sugar	5 mL
1	bay leaf	1
1/2 cup	sour cream	125 mL
	chopped parsley for garnish	

Heat the oven to 325°F (160°C).

Skin the chicken. Combine the flour and salt in a bowl and toss the chicken pieces in it until well coated. Melt the margarine in a skillet and lightly fry the onion 2 minutes. Add the chicken pieces and fry over medium heat until lightly browned on all sides. Remove and place in an ovenproof dish.

In the same skillet, combine the tomato juice, stock, paprika and sugar. Stir, scraping the bottom of the skillet well, and bring the mixture to a boil. Pour the sauce over the chicken. Add the bay leaf, cover the dish and bake until the chicken is tender, about 1 hour.

To serve, stir in the sour cream very lightly and sprinkle with parsley.

FRUITS AND CREAM WITH CURRIED COCONUT CHICKEN

Curries don't always have to be fiery. Here, pieces of chicken are baked gently in a mellow-flavoured sauce with the sweet taste of coconut. If fresh peaches aren't available, canned can be substituted. Serve with rice and a quick stir-fry of zucchini, onion and garlic. Serves 4.

1	3 1/2 lb. (1.75 kg) roasting chicken	1
2 tbsp.	butter or margarine	30 mL
1 tbsp.	vegetable oil	15 mL
1	medium onion, chopped	1
1	large clove garlic, crushed	1
1 tbsp.	curry powder	15 mL
2 tbsp.	all-purpose flour	30 mL
1 1/2 cups	chicken stock or broth	375 mL
2 tbsp.	red currant jelly	30 mL
4 tbsp.	coconut cream	60 mL
4 tbsp.	whipping cream	60 mL
1	peach or nectarine, peeled and sliced	1
1	banana, peeled and cut in long slices	1
	chopped parsley for garnish	

Heat the oven to 325°F (160°C). Skin the chicken and cut it into serving-size pieces. Melt the butter with the oil in a large skillet and fry the chicken over medium heat until brown on all sides. Remove and place in a casserole dish.

In the same skillet, sauté the onion and garlic over medium heat until the onion is lightly browned. Stir in the curry powder and cook for 30 seconds. Stir in the flour and cook a further 30 seconds. Stir in the stock gradually and bring the mixture to a boil, stirring until it thickens. Add the red currant jelly and simmer 2 minutes until dissolved. Stir in the coconut cream. Pour the sauce over the chicken, cover and bake 1 hour or until the chicken is cooked.

Remove the casserole from the oven and stir in the cream with the peach and banana. Return to the oven, covered, for a further 5 minutes. Serve sprinkled with a little parsley.

STIR-FRY CHICKEN AND VEGETABLES

The beauty of this classic Chinese-style recipe is that you can toss in any combination of your favourite fresh vegetables, or substitute shelled uncooked prawns for the chicken. The stir-fry method locks in the flavours and natural goodness of the ingredients. Serve it over long-grain rice and garnish with cherry tomatoes. Serves 1-2.

2 tbsp.	chicken stock, canned broth or dry sherry	30 mL
2 tsp.	soy sauce	10 mL
1 tsp.	chopped fresh ginger	5 mL
1	clove garlic, crushed	1
1	whole boneless chicken breast, skinned and cut into strips or chunks	1
1-2 tbsp.	oil	15-30 mL
2 cups	vegetables, cut up into small pieces (any combination of broccoli, red, orange, or green bell peppers, mushrooms, onions, celery, snow peas, zucchini)	500 mL
4 tbsp.	chicken stock or canned broth	60 mL
1 tbsp.	Worcestershire sauce	15 mL
	salt and pepper to taste	

In a glass bowl, mix together the 2 tbsp. (30 mL) of chicken stock (or sherry), soy sauce, ginger and garlic. Add the chicken pieces and marinate for 30 minutes. (If marinating any longer, refrigerate.)

Heat the oil in a wok or large skillet. Add the chicken and stir-fry over medium heat for 3-4 minutes. Remove and set aside on a warm plate. Add your chosen vegetables and sauté for 4-5 minutes. Add the 4 tbsp. (60 mL) chicken stock and Worcestershire sauce and season to taste. Let boil briefly.

Add the chicken to the pan and heat it through. Serve the stir-fry over rice and garnish with cherry tomatoes.

CHICKEN ORIENTAL

Microwave cooked chicken is always tender and moist, and when you marinate it first in this unique combination of sweet and spicy ingredients, it's even better. Serve it with piping hot rice or noodles, and a cool, crunchy cucumber and dill salad topped with sour cream dressing. Serves 8.

2 1/2 - 3 1/2 lbs.	chicken pieces	1.25 - 1.75 kg
4 tbsp.	soy sauce	60 mL
4 tbsp.	cooking sherry or apple juice	60 mL
1	clove garlic, crushed	1
1/2 tsp.	curry powder	2 mL
1/4 tsp.	dry mustard	1 mL
2 tbsp.	teriyaki sauce	30 mL
1 1/2 cups	plum jam	375 mL

Arrange the chicken pieces skin side down in a shallow microproof dish. Blend together the remaining ingredients in a 4 cup (1 L) microproof measure. Microwave on MEDIUM 50% power 4-6 minutes until jam is dissolved.

Allow the marinade to cool and pour it over the chicken pieces. Cover and refrigerate 4-6 hours, or overnight.

To cook, drain off and reserve the excess marinade. Turn the chicken skin side up, arranging the thicker portions towards the outside edge of the dish. Coat chicken generously with the reserved marinade. Cover the dish with waxed paper and microwave on MEDIUM HIGH 70% power 10 minutes. Rearrange the chicken pieces and coat them with any remaining marinade.

Cover the dish again and microwave on MEDIUM HIGH 70% power for a further 10-15 minutes.

Let stand, covered with foil, for 5-10 minutes before serving.

NDONESIAN NASI GORENG

Aromatic spices, tender strips of chicken and delicate shrimp make this Indonesian rice dish perfect for a dinner party or buffet. Serve a fresh tomato salad as a colourful accompaniment. Serves 4.

1 cup	long-grain rice	250 mL
2 tbsp.	vegetable oil	30 mL
2	shallots, chopped fine	2
1	large clove garlic, crushed	1
1	small fresh red chile pepper, seeded, chopped fine	1
1	boneless whole chicken breast, skinned and cut in thin strips	1
1 tbsp.	margarine or butter	15 mL
1 tsp.	ground coriander	5 mL
1 tsp.	curry powder	5 mL
1/2 tsp.	turmeric	2 mL
1/2 tsp.	caraway seeds	2 mL
2 tbsp.	soy sauce	30 mL
1/4 lb.	fresh shrimp, shelled, or frozen shrimp, thawed	125 g
1 cup	cooked peas	250 mL

Cook the rice in boiling water until tender, about 10 minutes. Drain it in a sieve, rinse under hot water and set aside.

Heat the oil in a large skillet and fry the shallots, garlic and chile over medium heat for 2-3 minutes until soft but not brown. Add the chicken and stir-fry about 6 minutes until cooked. Melt the margarine (or butter) in a separate skillet. Stir in the coriander, curry, turmeric, and caraway seeds and cook 1 minute. Stir in the soy sauce and shrimp, then the rice and peas.

Blend thoroughly, heat through and serve immediately.

INDONESIAN CHICKEN SATÉ WITH PEANUT SAUCE

Anyone sampling Indonesian cuisine for the first time is at once addicted to these delicious skewers of grilled meat with a robust peanut sauce. Serves 4.

2	whole boneless chicken breasts, skinned and cut into 3/4 inch (2 cm) cubes	2
1	clove garlic, crushed	1
1/2 tsp.	curry powder	2 mL
1/2 tsp.	cumin powder	2 mL
1/2 tsp.	chili powder	2 mL
1 tbsp.	lime or lemon juice	15 mL
2 tbsp.	soy sauce	30 mL
4 tbsp.	chicken bouillon, broth or stock	60 mL
14-16	bamboo skewers, 6 inches (15 cm) long, soaked in water for 20 minutes	14-16
	Peanut Sauce (recipe follows)	
	lime wedges and chopped green onion for garnish	

Place the chicken in a shallow bowl. Combine the garlic, curry, cumin, chili powder, lime juice, soy sauce and chicken bouillon. Pour over the chicken and marinate, covered, in the refrigerator for 1-2 hours, turning occasionally.

Remove the chicken from the marinade, reserving the marinade, and thread 4-5 pieces of meat onto each skewer. Broil it on a broiling rack, 6 inches (15 cm) away from the heat, for 12-15 minutes, until the meat is cooked. Turn each skewer halfway through the cooking time. Serve the saté on a bed of rice and garnish it with lime and green onion. Pour the Peanut Sauce in individual small bowls for dipping.

PEANUT SAUCE

2 tbsp.	vegetable oil	30 mL
2	shallots, chopped fine	2
1 tbsp.	brown sugar	15 mL
1/3 cup	smooth or crunchy peanut butter	75 mL
2/3 cup	water	150 mL
3 tbsp.	whipping cream	45 mL

The Easy Gourmet features a photograph of this recipe on the front cover.

While the meat is cooking, heat the oil in a small pan and sauté the shallots until soft but not brown. Strain in the reserved marinade and stir in the sugar, peanut butter, water and cream. Bring to a boil, stirring, and cook, stirring, about 2 minutes or until the sauce thickens.

SAUTÉ OF CHICKEN WITH A HERBED WINE SAUCE

Fresh herbs and a julienne of tender-crisp vegetables are the secret of this easy, elegant dish. A simple rice pilaf sets it off perfectly. Serves 8.

4 tbsp.	butter	60 mL
2 tbsp.	oil	30 mL
4	whole boneless chicken breasts, halved, or	4
8	thighs, boned	8
4	leeks, white part only, thinly sliced to make a julienne	4
4	carrots, sliced to same thickness as leeks	4
1 1/4 cups (10 oz.)	chicken stock or canned broth	284 mL
1 cup	whipping cream	250 mL
4 tbsp.	fresh herbs, such as cilantro or parsley	60 mL
	salt and pepper to taste	

Heat the butter and oil in a large skillet until very hot. Add the chicken, skin side down, and reduce heat to medium-high. Sauté until golden, about 5 minutes. Turn and sauté the other side for 2-3 minutes. Remove from the pan and set aside. Reduce the heat to medium and sauté the leeks and carrots for 2-3 minutes in the same pan. Add the stock, reduce the heat and simmer until the vegetables are tender-crisp, about 5 minutes. If prepared ahead, refrigerate at this point.

To serve, reheat the vegetables in the cooking liquid and add the chicken. Cover with a lid or foil and steam for 3-5 minutes or until the chicken is done. Remove the chicken and vegetables to heated serving plates.

Bring the cooking liquid to a boil and boil until reduced by half. Add the cream and bring to boiling again. Boil, stirring, until the mixture reaches a sauce-like consistency. Add the herbs and seasonings. Spoon generously over the chicken and pass the extra sauce.

CHICKEN LASAGNE

Looking for a change of pace? This lasagne variation calls for cream cheese, cottage cheese and the classic broad noodles, all bathed in a creamy chicken and mushroom sauce. It freezes well, and it's just as good when you use leftover cooked turkey. Add a deep green romaine salad with a simple vinaigrette and some warm Italian bread, and you have a dinner to remember. Serves 6-8.

1	8 oz. (250 g) pkg. lasagne noodles	1
1	10 oz. (284 mL) can cream of mushroom soup	1
1 cup	milk	250 mL
1/2 cup	chicken stock or canned broth	125 mL
1/4 lb.	fresh mushrooms, sliced	125 g
1/2 tsp.	freshly ground black pepper	2 mL
1/2 tsp.	poultry seasoning	2 mL
1	8 oz. (250 g) pkg. cream cheese, at room temperature	1
1	8 oz. (250 g) carton cottage cheese, any type	1
1/2 cup	chopped stuffed olives	125 mL
1/2 cup	chopped celery	125 mL
1/2 cup	chopped green bell pepper	125 mL
4 tbsp.	chopped green onions	60 mL
4 tbsp.	minced parsley	60 mL
4 cups	diced cooked chicken (note: one whole breast yields about 1 1/2 cups (375 mL) meat)	1 L
1 1/2 cups	fine dry bread crumbs	375 mL
4 tbsp.	melted butter	60 mL

Cook the lasagne noodles in boiling water. While the lasagne is cooking, mix together the soup, milk, chicken stock, mushrooms and seasonings in a medium saucepan. Heat to boiling. Remove from the heat and set aside. Drain the lasagne and set aside.

Beat together the cream cheese and cottage cheese until well blended. Stir in the olives, celery, green pepper, green onions and parsley. Set aside.

Heat the oven to 375°F (190°C). Grease a 9 x 13 inch (23 x 32 cm/4 L) baking dish. Place half the cooked noodles in the dish. Top with half the cheese mixture, half the cooked chicken and half the soup mixture. Repeat the layers.

Combine the crumbs with the melted butter and sprinkle over all. Bake until bubbling and lightly browned, about 40 minutes.

CHICKEN THIGHS WITH PEANUT SAUCE

There is a hint of Indonesia in every bite of this unusual main dish—bathed in a sauce of crunchy peanut butter, green onion, tomato and heady spices, and baked to a bubbly finish. This dish takes minutes to assemble, and only 40 minutes to bake, leaving time to assemble a crunchy raw carrot salad, a platter of crisp vegetables, and a pot full of fluffy steamed rice. Serves 3.

6	chicken thighs	6
1	10 oz. (284 mL) can chicken broth	1
2 tbsp.	crunchy peanut butter	30 mL
2 tbsp.	oil	30 mL
2	green onions, chopped	2
2	medium tomatoes, seeded and chopped	2
1	clove garlic, crushed	1
pinch	cayenne pepper or to taste	pinch

Heat the oven to 350°F (180°C). Grease a shallow baking dish. Place the chicken in the prepared dish. Mix together the remaining ingredients and pour them over the chicken.

Bake until the chicken is cooked and the juices are bubbling, about 40 minutes. Baste once or twice during the cooking time.

C HICKEN WITH CINNAMON AND FRUIT

An exotic combination of flavours makes this a memorable dish that is even better the next day—if you have any leftovers! Give it centre stage, accompanied by warm butterflake rolls and a bright green tossed salad. Serves 8.

4 1/2 lbs.	chicken (or turkey) pieces	2.25 kg
6	peppercorns	6
1	whole clove	1
1/2 inch	piece of cinnamon stick	1 cm
1 tbsp.	sugar	15 mL
4 tbsp.	apple juice or sherry	60 mL
3	cloves garlic, chopped	3
4 tbsp.	vinegar	60 mL
1	large white onion, thinly sliced	1
2	medium tomatoes, thinly sliced	2
1	*each* small apple and pear, peeled, cored and thinly sliced	1
1	bay leaf	1
pinch	dried oregano	pinch
pinch	dried thyme	pinch
	capers and olives for garnish	

Heat oven to 375°F (190°C). Grind together the peppercorns, clove and cinnamon. Mix with the sugar, apple juice, garlic and vinegar. Set aside.

Spread about a third of the onion on the bottom of a 4 quart (4 L) casserole with a lid. Cover with a third each of the tomato slices and fruits. Add the bay leaf and sprinkle with a half each of the oregano and thyme. Arrange half the chicken pieces on top and pour half the vinegar/spice mixture on top. Repeat with a third each of the onion, tomatoes and fruit, and the rest of the herbs. Cover with the remaining chicken and the rest of the vinegar mixture. Top with the remaining onions and fruit.

Cover the casserole and bake for 1 hour. Uncover and bake until the chicken is tender and the juices reduce a little, about 30 minutes.

MEDITERRANEAN BRAISED TURKEY THIGHS

Turkey thighs are a plump, succulent cut, readily available year-round and so versatile and simple to prepare. This version, Mediterranean-inspired, gets a quick 15-minute browning and assembly, and the oven does the rest. Serve with hot garlicky bread, a fresh green salad, and saffron rice or pasta. Serves 4-6.

2 tbsp.	olive oil	30 mL
4	turkey thighs, about 3 lbs (1.5 kg)	4
	salt and pepper	
1	onion, cut into thin slivers	1
2	red bell peppers, de-ribbed, seeded and cut into thin slivers	2
2	large cloves garlic, slivered	2
2 cups	prepared marinara or pasta suace (your favourite brand)	500 mL
3 tbsp.	raisins	45 mL
1/3 cup	capers, rinsed	75 mL
1/2 cup	cured kalamata olives	125 mL
2 tbsp.	finely minced fresh parsley	30 mL

Heat the olive oil in a large skillet over medium-high heat. Brown the turkey thighs 5 minutes per side, turning once and seasoning with salt and pepper. Place the thighs in a single layer in a deep ovenproof baking dish with a cover.

Heat the oven to 350°F (180°C). Add the onions, peppers and garlic to the drippings in the skillet. Sauté, stirring, until the vegetables soften slightly and just begin to colour. Scatter the vegetables over the turkey. Gently heat the marinara sauce in the skillet for 3-4 minutes, and add the raisins, capers and olives. Pour the sauce over the turkey and vegetables. Cover the baking dish.

Bake for 2 1/2 hours, or until the turkey is fork-tender. Remove it from the oven and transfer the turkey and vegetables to a warm platter. If the sauce is too thin, reduce the juices over high heat for 4-5 minutes until thickened and syrupy. Pour over the turkey, and serve hot or warm.

The Easy Gourmet features a photograph of this recipe on page 89.

J UICY TURKEY BURGERS WITH RED PEPPER PESTO

Ground turkey is a wonderful choice for hearty, thick broiled or pan-fried supper burgers. Serve these burgers open-faced on grilled sourdough rounds, or tuck them into toasted onion buns. Top with a generous spoonful of Red Pepper Pesto. A colourful pasta salad is a nice accompaniment, alongside a plate of crisp raw vegetables. Serves 4.

1 1/2 lbs.	ground turkey	750 g
4 oz.	ham, finely minced or ground (with some fat, to provide moisture for the burgers)	125 g
1/2 cup	*each* chopped black ripe olives, green bell pepper and onion	125 mL
1/2 tsp.	*each* dried thyme, sage and oregano, crumbled	1 mL
1	egg, lightly beaten	1
1/3 cup	fresh bread crumbs	75 mL
2 tbsp.	vegetable oil	30 mL
	Red Pepper Pesto (recipe follows)	

Combine the turkey, ham, olives, green pepper, onion, thyme, sage, oregano, egg and bread crumbs. Knead gently, but thoroughly, for several minutes to bind the ingredients. Form the mixture into 4 thick patties, flattening them slightly into 3/4-inch (2 cm) thick rounds. Cover loosely, and refrigerate 1-2 hours to firm and allow flavours to blend.

In a hot skillet, pan-fry the burgers in the oil until crusty on the outside and cooked through but still juicy on the inside. Pierce the meat to make sure that the juices run clear, with no trace of pink. The finished burgers will feel just firm when pressed. Total cooking time will be approximately 6-7 minutes per side.

Serve the burgers piping hot, each napped with a generous spoonful of Red Pepper Pesto.

RED PEPPER PESTO

1	large clove garlic, chopped	1
1 tsp.	salt	5 mL
1 cup	blanched almonds, toasted pale golden in a 325°F (160°C) oven 10 minutes, cooled	250 mL
1 tsp.	sugar	5 mL
1	16-oz. (450 mL) jar roasted whole red peppers, packed in brine, drained and patted dry	1
2 tsp.	sherry vinegar or red wine vinegar	10 mL
2/3 cup	olive oil	150 mL

Process the garlic and salt to a paste in a food processor or with a mortar and pestle. Add the almonds, and process until very finely ground. If you are not using a food processor, place the mixture in a blender at this point. Add the sugar and red peppers, and process until the mixture is a smooth, grainy pureé. Add the vinegar, and combine. With the motor running, add the olive oil in a slow, thin, steady stream. The finished pesto should be like grainy mayonnaise.

Transfer the sauce to a jar with a tight-fitting lid. Cap tightly, and chill overnight for the best flavour. The sauce may be stored up to one week. Serve it cool or at room temperature.

TURKEY IN SPICY MANGO CREAM

This is a special treat for two that is easy to prepare. Thin slices of turkey are quickly fried, then coated in a creamy mango sauce with a hint of curry. As an accompaniment, steamed snow peas or asparagus sprinkled with toasted almonds would add to the occasion. Serves 2.

2	turkey cutlets, about 1/4 lb. (125 g) each	2
1 1/2 tbsp.	margarine or butter	25 mL
1 tsp.	mustard seeds	5 mL
1/2 tsp.	curry powder	2 mL
1/2 cup	whipping cream or half-and-half cream	125 mL
2 tbsp.	mango chutney	30 mL
1/2	small red bell pepper, cored, seeded and cut in thin strips	1/2
	kiwi slices for garnish	

Heat the oven to 350°F (180°C).

Cut each turkey cutlet into quarters. Place each piece between two sheets of waxed paper and beat with a wooden mallet or rolling pin to half the original thickness.

Melt the margarine in a skillet and sauté the turkey 4-5 minutes, turning occasionally until lightly browned on both sides. Remove the turkey and place it in a shallow casserole dish.

Add the mustard seeds and curry powder to the skillet and fry, stirring, for 30 seconds. Deglaze the skillet by pouring in the cream over medium heat and scraping the bottom of the pan. Stir in the chutney and red pepper and pour the sauce over the turkey. Cover and bake for 15 minutes.

To serve, arrange the turkey slices on a warmed serving platter. Pour sauce over them and garnish with kiwi.

Opposite: (Top to bottom) Turkey and Prosciutto Saltimbocca (page 98); Mediterranean Braised Turkey Thighs (page 85).

STUFFED TURKEY ROAST

Turkey cooked in the microwave stays moist and full of flavour, so you can serve a lovely traditional holiday dinner—or a very special everyday dinner—in a fraction of the time. Don't forget the trimmings! Serves 8.

2 lbs.	boneless turkey roast	1 kg
1 cup	all-purpose stuffing mix	250 mL
1/2 cup	chopped pitted prunes	125 mL
1	tart apple, peeled, cored and finely chopped	1
1/2 cup	chicken broth (homemade or canned)	125 mL
4 tbsp.	melted butter	60 mL
1 tsp.	paprika	5 mL

Place the turkey skin side down and flatten the thicker parts of the meat with a meat mallet.

Combine the stuffing mix, prunes and apple. Bring the chicken broth to a boil on HIGH 100% power and blend it into the stuffing mix with 2 tbsp. (30 mL) of the melted butter.

Spread the stuffing mix evenly over the prepared turkey. Fold the meat over the stuffing so that the skin side is on top. Tie with a string in 3 or 4 places to make an even-shaped roll.

Place the turkey in a shallow microproof dish. Combine the remaining melted butter with the paprika and brush over the skin surface of the turkey.

Microwave on MEDIUM HIGH 70% power, allowing 11-13 minutes per pound. Allow to stand, covered, for about 10 minutes before slicing. For a traditional browned look, heat the broiler of a conventional oven and broil the roast for 10 minutes. Slice, serve, and enjoy!

TURKEY TAMALE PIE

This hearty south-of-the-border casserole is utterly delicious—full of Mexican flavours and loaded with chunks of turkey. Serve it with a leafy green salad dressed in a vinaigrette, and pitchers of cool iced tea or beer. Serves 6-8.

1/2 cup + 1 tbsp.	corn oil	140 mL
1	medium-large onion, chopped	1
1	green bell pepper, seeded and de-ribbed, chopped	1
1 1/2 tbsp.	chili powder	25 mL
1/3 cup	dried currants or raisins, rinsed and drained	75 mL
1	28 oz. (796 mL) can chopped Italian plum tomatoes, with juices	1
1	14 oz. (398 mL) can cream-style corn	1
1 tbsp.	salt	15 mL
1/2 tsp.	black pepper	2 mL
3	eggs, lightly beaten	3
1/2 cup	*each* milk and half-and-half cream	125 mL
2/3 cup	yellow corn meal	150 mL
1/2 cup	*each* sliced pitted black olives and sliced pitted green olives	125 mL
4 tbsp.	finely minced fresh parsley	60 mL
2 1/2 cups	cooked turkey or chicken, coarsely chopped	625 mL
1 cup	grated Cheddar cheese	250 mL

Heat 1/2 cup (125 mL) of the oil in a deep, heavy saucepan and add the onion and green pepper. Sauté, stirring, until tender and pale golden. Add the chili powder and currants (or raisins), and sauté 2 minutes until the ingredients are blended and the currants are plumped. Add the tomatoes, corn, salt and pepper. Heat the mixture until bubbly and slightly thickened, about 12 minutes.

Combine the eggs, milk, cream and corn meal, whisking to a smooth mixture. Slowly add it to the tomato mixture, stirring, and heat through over low (to prevent scorching) heat about 10 minutes. Remove it from the heat, and allow to cool 20 minutes. Heat the oven to 350°F (180°C).

Lightly oil a 3 quart (3 L) shallow crockery baking dish. Gently combine the prepared tamale mixture with the black olives, green olives, and chopped turkey. Pour it into the prepared dish. Top with the grated cheese, and drizzle with the remaining 1 tbsp. (15 mL) oil.

Bake the pie about 40 minutes, until the filling is firmed and the top is a rich golden brown and crusty. Remove the pie from the oven and allow it to cool 15-20 minutes before serving.

Note: If you are serving the tamale pie for a party, you might like to decorate the top with additional sliced olives and sprigs of cilantro, and serve each helping with a dollop of sour cream.

URKEY ENCHILADAS "SUIZAS"

These creamy turkey and chile filled enchiladas are a snap to prepare, and are exotic enough for company fare. Serve with a garnish of avocado guacamole, a dollop of sour cream, thinly sliced radishes and green onions, and a sprig of fresh cilantro. Cool iced tea or a pitcher of fruit-laced sangría is the ideal accompaniment. Serves 4.

2 tbsp.	corn oil	30 mL
2 cups	thinly slivered onion (about 2 medium)	500 mL
1	red bell pepper, seeded and de-ribbed, cut into thin slivers	1
1 tsp.	*each* ground cumin and coriander	5 mL
2 cups	shredded cooked turkey (or chicken)	500 mL
1	4 oz. (114 mL) can diced roasted chiles	1
2	4 oz. (125 g) pkgs. cream cheese, diced	2
	corn oil for frying	
8	corn tortillas, 6 inches (15 cm) in diameter	8
1 cup	whipping cream	250 mL
1/2 cup	*each* shredded Swiss cheese and Monterey jack cheese	125 mL

Heat the 2 tbsp. (30 mL) corn oil in a skillet, and add the onion and red pepper slivers. Sauté over medium-high heat until just softened and pale golden on the edges. Stir in the cumin and coriander, and heat 2 minutes to flavour. Remove the mixture from the heat and stir in the cooked turkey (or chicken), chiles, and cream cheese. Stir the mixture with a fork to blend (the cream cheese does not have to be smooth).

Heat 1/2 inch (1 cm) corn oil in a non-stick skillet over medium heat. Dip each tortilla in the oil, holding it with tongs, for 6 seconds on each side to soften. Do not fry crisp! Drain the tortillas briefly, and place 1/3 cup (75 mL) of the filling down the centre of each one. Roll to enclose the filling, and place the filled tortillas seam side down in a 9 x 13 inch (23 x 32 cm) baking dish. Heat the oven to 375°F (190°C). Prepare and assemble the suggested garnishes. Pour cream evenly over the tops of the rolled enchiladas to moisten. Sprinkle the tops evenly with the grated cheeses.

Bake, uncovered, about 20-25 minutes, or until the enchiladas are heated through and the cheese is bubbly. Serve hot with guacamole, sour cream, sliced radishes, lime wedges, and sliced green onions. Garnish each one with a sprig of cilantro.

Note: Frozen, thawed avocado guacamole is quick and convenient.

SWEET AND SOUR TURKEY BAKE

This sweet and sour sauce will enhance turkey or any type of chicken. Just cut up the poultry into serving pieces, pour on the sauce and bake to create a new family favourite. Serve with a vegetable medley and dinner rolls. Serves 4.

3/4 cup	orange juice	175 mL
1 tbsp.	cornstarch	15 mL
1/3 cup	mango chutney	75 mL
2 tbsp.	cider vinegar	30 mL
2 tbsp.	brown sugar	30 mL
1	clove garlic, crushed	1
1 tsp.	*each* dried basil, ground cinnamon, ground nutmeg and ground ginger	5 mL
	salt and pepper to taste	
2 1/2 lbs.	turkey pieces	1.25 kg

In a small pot blend together the orange juice and cornstarch. Cook and stir over medium heat until it boils and thickens. Remove it from the heat and stir in the remaining ingredients. The sauce may be ahead to this point and refrigerated.

Heat the oven to 375°F (190°C). Place the turkey pieces in an ovenproof casserole. Spread on the sauce and bake, basting occasionally, until done, about 1 hour. Serve piping hot topped with any remaining sauce.

TURKEY SCALLOPINE WITH LEMON AND CAPERS

*This delicious version of the classic Veal Scallopine features turkey —
economical, widely available, and low in fat. Turkey turns this famous
dish into a festive everyday meal. Serve it with rice or pasta (try thin
spaghettini), sautéed zucchini or fresh spinach, and a loaf of crusty Italian
bread. Serves 4.*

1 lb.	turkey "scallops" (boneless turkey breast, sliced 1/8 inch (3 mm) thick into scallops)	500 g
2 tbsp.	olive oil	30 mL
7 tbsp.	butter	105 mL
	salt and freshly ground pepper	
2 tbsp.	tiny capers, drained	30 mL
3 tbsp.	fresh lemon juice	45 mL
1/2 cup	Marsala wine, dry sherry or chicken stock	125 mL
2 tbsp.	minced fresh parsley	30 mL
	thin lemon slices	

Pat the turkey scallops dry. Heat the oil and 4 tbsp. (60 mL) of the butter
in a large, heavy skillet over medium-high heat until the butter foams. Add
the scallops, and sauté very quickly, turning only once, until pale golden on
both sides, 2-3 minutes per side.

Season the scallops lightly with salt and pepper as they brown.

Remove the scallops to a warmed platter. Add the capers and lemon juice
to the skillet. Increase the heat to high, and deglaze the pan (stir up the
juices and browned bits clinging to the pan) for 2-3 minutes. Add the
Marsala (or sherry or chicken stock) and heat over high heat until very
bubbly and thickened, about 4-5 minutes. The sauce should lightly coat a
spoon.

Swirl in the remaining 3 tbsp. (45 mL) butter, 1 tbsp. (15 mL) at a time, to
finish the sauce. Stir in the parsley, heat 30 seconds, and pour the sauce
over the scallops. Garnish with thin slices of lemon and serve at once.

TURKEY PARMESAN, ITALIAN-STYLE

Anyone fond of Veal Parmesan will love this recipe. Economical, lower in fat, and quick to assemble—this is a perfect party dish with no fuss or hassle. The dish may be assembled several hours ahead of time and popped into the oven for the final 20-minute bake, while the pasta accompaniment is prepared. Serve with hot spaghetti, fusilli or linguine, fresh green beans, and a crusty hot loaf of garlic bread. Serves 6.

1 1/2 cups	bread crumbs, combined with	375 mL
1/2 cup	Parmesan cheese, grated	125 mL
1/2 tsp.	*each* salt, black pepper and nutmeg	2 mL
2 tsp.	*each* dried oregano and basil	10 mL
2 lbs.	turkey breast, sliced into scallops 1/3 inch (1 cm) thick, 3 inches (7.5 cm) wide	1 kg
2	eggs, beaten with 1 tbsp. (15 mL) water	2
1 cup	(or as needed) olive oil	250 mL
8 oz.	*each* thinly sliced Canadian round back bacon and Mozzarella cheese	250 g
6 tbsp.	marinara sauce (prepared, bottled sauce is great in this recipe)	90 mL
3 tbsp.	finely minced fresh parsley	45 mL

Combine the bread crumbs, Parmesan cheese, salt, pepper, nutmeg, oregano and basil. Dip each turkey scallop into the egg-wash, then coat lightly with the crumb mixture. Heat the olive oil in a very large non-stick skillet over medium-high heat, and fry the breaded scallops, a few at a time, 2-3 minutes per side or until golden brown on both sides.

Oil the bottom and sides of an ovenproof baking dish (porcelain or crockery is ideal), and arrange the browned scallops in a single layer. Top each scallop with 1 slice of bacon, and cover each with a slice of cheese. Finally, top each with 1-2 tbsp. (15-30 mL) of marinara sauce.

Heat the oven to 350°F (180°C). Bake the assembled dish 20-30 minutes, or until the cheese is melted and bubbly, and pale golden brown. Serve piping hot.

TURKEY AND PROSCIUTTO SALTIMBOCCA

The classic "Saltimbocca," literally translated from the Italian, means "jump in the mouth." It's that good! This version calls for economical turkey scallopine, and the results are delicious. This is company fare, so serve it with pasta or a mushroom risotto, braised fresh green chard or spinach, and a Belgian endive salad. Serves 4.

1 lb.	turkey "scallops" (boneless turkey breast, sliced 1/4 inch (6 mm) thick into scallops), 8 total	500 g
	salt, pepper and ground nutmeg	
1	bunch fresh sage leaves	1
8	slices prosciutto	8
2 tbsp.	olive oil	30 mL
4 tbsp.	butter	60 mL
4 tbsp.	finely minced shallots	60 mL
2 tbsp.	fresh lemon juice	30 mL
1/2 cup	dry white wine, vermouth or chicken stock	125 mL
1 tbsp.	very finely minced fresh sage	15 mL
2 tbsp.	finely minced fresh parsley	30 mL
1/2 cup	whipping cream	125 mL
	fresh sage leaves	

Between waxed paper sheets, pound the turkey scallops slightly to flatten. Season each pounded scallop lightly with salt, pepper and nutmeg. Press 1 large sage leaf or several smaller leaves on top of each scallop, and top each with 1 slice prosciutto to cover. Press lightly, fastening each with a toothpick if needed.

Heat the oil and butter in a large, heavy skillet over medium-high heat until the butter foams. Add the prepared scallops (prosciutto side up), and sauté 3-4 minutes until golden. Turn and sauté 1-2 minutes until the prosciutto edges curl.

The Easy Gourmet features a photograph of this recipe on page 89.

Remove the scallops to a warmed platter. Add the shallots to the pan drippings, and sauté 2 minutes, stirring. Add the lemon juice and wine (or stock), increase the heat to high, and deglaze the pan (stir up all the juices and browned bits clinging to it). Cook until the liquid is reduced by half and is thickened and syrupy, about 4-5 minutes. Stir in the sage, parsley and cream. Heat over high heat 2-3 minutes, stirring, until bubbly and thickened. Taste and correct the seasoning.

Partially cover each "saltimbocca" with a spoonful of sauce, and garnish with fresh sprigs of sage. Serve at once, piping hot.

 URKEY SCHNITZEL

If you've never tried minced turkey, this is the recipe to start with. Delicately garnished with lemon twists and fresh parsley, it's a family favourite next to mixed vegetables and mashed potatoes with gravy. Serves 4-6.

1 lb.	ground or minced turkey	500 g
4 tbsp.	all-purpose flour	60 mL
2	eggs, beaten	2
1 cup	fine dry bread crumbs	250 mL
1 tsp.	freshly ground black pepper	5 mL
1 tsp.	paprika	5 mL
pinch	salt	pinch
2 tbsp.	oil	30 mL
2 tbsp.	butter	30 mL
	lemon and parsley for garnish	

Shape the minced turkey into six patties, about 1/3 cup (75 mL) each. Place the flour on a flat plate and the eggs in a shallow bowl. Mix together the bread crumbs, pepper, paprika and salt and spread the mixture on a flat plate. Coat the patties with flour, dip them into the beaten egg and then into the crumb mixture. Place on a sheet of waxed paper.

Heat the oil and butter in a medium skillet over medium heat. Cook the turkey patties until golden on both sides, about 5 minutes on each side.

Place the schnitzel on a serving platter and garnish with twists of lemon and sprinkles of chopped parsley. Serve hot.

ROAST DUCK WITH TANGY CITRUS SAUCE

Roast duck is always cause for a special celebration, and this version—roasted crispy on the outside, and melt-in-your-mouth tender on the inside—gets a special citrus sauce based on the classic Cumberland recipe. Accompany with fresh steamed broccoli and carrots, and wild rice studded with toasted pecans and currants. Serves 4.

1	duck, about 3 lbs. (1.5 kg)	1
	salt and pepper	

TANGY CITRUS SAUCE:

3	medium oranges	3
1	lemon	1
1 tbsp.	sugar	15 mL
1 tbsp.	vinegar	15 mL
2 tbsp.	red wine	30 mL
4 tbsp.	red currant jelly	60 mL
1 tbsp.	cornstarch	15 mL
	orange slices and watercress for garnish	

Heat the oven to 375°F (190°C).

Place the duck in a roasting pan and prick the skin all over with a skewer to help release fat as the duck roasts. Sprinkle the duck with salt and pepper. Bake, uncovered, until the duck is cooked and the skin is golden and crisp, 1 3/4 - 2 hours. Drain off excess fat occasionally. Cut the duck into serving-size pieces and arrange them on a serving platter. Cover and keep warm. Pour off all but 1 tbsp. (15 mL) fat from the roasting pan and set the pan aside.

To make the sauce, finely grate the rind of 1 orange, avoiding the bitter pith, and squeeze the juice from all the oranges (about 2/3 cup [150 mL]) and the lemon. Strain the juices. In a small, heavy-based pan over low heat, dissolve the sugar in the vinegar. Turn the heat to high and allow to cook, without stirring, until the mixture turns a dark caramel colour. Watch it constantly so that it does not burn. Remove it from the heat and pour in the wine, orange and lemon juices. The mixture may solidify when the liquid is added. Add the red currant jelly and orange rind and cook, stirring over medium heat, until the mixture is dissolved.

Place the roasting pan over medium heat. Stir the cornstarch into the reserved fat and cook, stirring, for 1 minute, scraping the bottom of the pan. Gradually pour in the orange juice mixture and bring to a boil, stirring, until the mixture thickens. Season to taste with salt and pepper. Pour the sauce over the duck and garnish with orange slices and watercress.

MAPLE GLAZED CORNISH HENS

Microwave cooking is just perfect for Cornish hens, because it helps to retain the natural moisture and tenderness during cooking. The maple and apple flavours of the glaze in this recipe complement the delicate quality of the meat. Serve it all up next to well-seasoned white and wild rice studded with fresh mushrooms and assorted steamed fresh vegetables. Serves 4.

2	Cornish game hens, approx. 1 lb. (500 g) each	2
1	small onion, halved	1
1	small apple, peeled and quartered	1
1/2 cup	maple syrup	125 mL
1/2 cup	apple jelly	125 mL
1/2 tsp.	salt	2 mL
1/4 tsp.	poultry seasoning	1 mL

Place one onion half and two apple quarters in the cavity of each hen. Truss the wings and drumsticks with fine string.

Combine the remaining ingredients in a 2 cup (500 mL) microproof measure. Microwave on MEDIUM 50% power 2-4 minutes until the jelly is dissolved. Brush each hen generously with the glaze mixture.

Place the hens breast side down in a shallow microproof dish. Cover with waxed paper. Microwave on HIGH 100% power, allowing 6-8 minutes per pound (500 g), for one half of the required cooking time.

Turn the hens breast side up. Brush each hen generously with the glaze mixture. Cover with waxed paper and microwave on HIGH 100% power for the second half of the cooking time.

Brush with the remaining glaze, cover with foil and let stand 10 minutes. The hens are done when the leg moves freely and the juices run clear when the inner thigh is pierced with a fork.

To serve, remove the string. Remove the apple and onion from the cavities and discard. Split each hen in half.

RABBIT IN MUSTARD SAUCE

Try rabbit—a tender meat reminiscent of chicken, that lends itself to most chicken recipes. The classical French dish of lapin à la moutarde (rabbit in mustard sauce) is a hearty, rich stew spiked with local Dijon mustard. Serve this elegant dish with mashed potatoes, fresh carrots, and bright green beans cloaked in butter. Serves 4.

3 lbs.	frozen rabbit pieces, thawed	1.5 kg
4 tbsp.	butter	60 mL
2 tbsp.	oil	30 mL
3/4 cup	chopped onion	175 mL
1	clove garlic, minced	1
1 1/2 cups	chicken stock or canned broth	375 mL
3/4 cup	whipping cream	175 mL
1/2 cup	dry white wine or	125 mL
	non-alcoholic white wine	
1 sprig	*each* fresh parsley, thyme and bay leaf	1 sprig
4 tbsp.	Dijon mustard	60 mL
3	egg yolks	3
	salt and pepper to taste	

Pat the rabbit pieces dry. Heat the butter and oil and brown the rabbit pieces over medium heat. Remove the meat from the pan and add the onion. Sauté until tender. Add the garlic and cook another minute. Pour in the chicken stock, cream and wine and bring to a boil. Return the rabbit to the pan along with the herbs. Reduce the heat and simmer until the rabbit is tender, about 20 minutes. Place the rabbit on a warm platter and keep warm.

Strain the cooking juices into a small saucepan and bring to a boil. Mix together the mustard and egg yolks. Slowly stir some of the hot juices into the mustard mixture. Reduce the heat under the saucepan to medium and stir in the thinned mustard mixture. Whisk and cook until the mixture thickens to a medium gravy. Season to taste.

Place the rabbit on serving plates and spoon on the sauce.

SEAFOOD

Today's sophisticated transport and storage methods truly bring the sea to your kitchen, and Safeway offers a wonderful array of fresh, frozen and canned fish. In these pages are recipes ranging from the tried and true—B.C. Salmon Soufflé or Trout Amandine—to the truly exotic—Cajun Crabcakes and Wraparound Prawns on Sweet and Sour Sauce.

HALIBUT IN LIME MARINADE

Halibut and other firm white fish (try swordfish or shark as a variation) take well to marinades, and the flavours are absorbed very quickly. Try this Mexican-influenced recipe, equally good whether you're broiling or grilling the fish. Serve it with a sauté of fresh mushrooms and a platter of hash browns spiked with onion and bell peppers. Serves 4.

	juice of 3 limes	
1/2 cup	olive oil	125 mL
3/4 cup	finely chopped fresh cilantro	175 mL
4	medium fish steaks, 1 inch (2.5 cm) thick	4
4 tbsp.	unsalted butter, softened	60 mL
	lime wedges and chopped cilantro for garnish	

Mix together the lime juice, olive oil and cilantro. Spread the mixture over the fish and marinate in a shallow dish for not more than 30 minutes, turning occasionally.

Grill or broil the fish, basting occasionally with the marinade, until done: about 10 minutes per inch (2.5 cm) measured at the thickest part of the fish. Turn the fish after 5 minutes of cooking time.

Spread the butter over the hot steaks. Sprinkle with cilantro and decorate with lime wedges.

The Easy Gourmet features a photograph of this recipe on page 107.

QUICK BAKED HALIBUT FOR ONE (OR MORE!)

Here is a simple, delicious dinner for seafood lovers: halibut baked with sour cream, mayonnaise, tomato and the added surprise of a sprinkle of mint. Try it with salmon, sole, snapper, cod—whatever is fresh. A plate of raw vegetables with sour cream dip and a basket of whole wheat dinner rolls make this a perfect-tasting, perfectly simple dinner.

For each serving:

1	portion of fish	1
1 tbsp.	mayonnaise	15 mL
1 tbsp.	sour cream	15 mL
	chopped fresh mint	
	3-4 slices of fresh tomato	
	freshly ground black pepper	
	chopped parsley	

Heat the oven to 425°F (220°C).

Place each serving of fish in the centre of a square of lightly greased foil or parchment, 8 x 8 inches (20 x 20 cm). Mix together the mayonnaise and sour cream and spread over the fish. Top with a generous sprinkling of chopped mint, the slices of tomato, a few grinds of fresh pepper and some chopped parsley.

Fold in the edges of the foil to form a sealed package for each serving. Place on a baking sheet and bake for 15 minutes.

Place each foil package on a serving plate and tear them open—wonderful aromas will waft upwards. Eat them right from the package.

RANGE-WALNUT COD

The delightfully different combination of flavours and textures in this dish brings a festive touch to dinner. Cooked in the microwave, it's quick and perfect every time. Try substituting halibut or snapper for the cod, and serve it with silver dollar fries (in the freezer section) and a bright green vegetable. Serves 4.

2 tbsp.	butter	30 mL
1/2 cup	chopped onion	125 mL
1	l lb. (500 g) cod fillet	1
dash	salt	dash
dash	white pepper	dash
	juice of 1 orange	
	grated rind of 1 orange	
2	oranges, peeled and segmented	2
1/2 cup	walnut pieces	125 mL
	watercress or parsley for garnish	

Place the butter and onion in a shallow microproof dish. Cover with plastic wrap and microwave on HIGH 100% power 2-3 minutes until onion is soft.

Cut the cod fillet into equal serving-size pieces. Place skin side down on the butter/onion mixture, making sure the thicker edges are towards the outside edge of the dish. Sprinkle orange juice over the fish and season lightly with salt and pepper.

Cover the dish with plastic wrap, vent the edge and microwave on HIGH 100% power 4-6 minutes until the fish is opaque.

Mix together the orange rind, orange segments and walnuts. Season lightly with salt and pepper and spread equal amounts on the pieces of fish. Cover and microwave on HIGH 100% power for a further 2-3 minutes until the orange segments are heated through.

Serve garnished with watercress or parsley sprigs.

Opposite: (Top to bottom) Halibut in Lime Marinade (page 104); Quick Crab Bisque (page 132); Blackened Salmon Fillets with Fresh Citrus Butter (page 116).

MOKED COD KEDGEREE

Kedgeree is an English breakfast dish of East Indian origin, served in the days when people had time to linger over their first meal of the day. Now it is more commonly served as a lunch or supper dish, for which this recipe has been adapted. A tossed green salad makes a refreshing accompaniment. Serves 4.

1 lb.	smoked cod	500 g
1 cup	uncooked long-grain rice	250 mL
2	leeks, washed and sliced	2
4 tbsp.	butter or margarine	60 mL
1/2 tsp.	ground turmeric	2 mL
2 tsp.	dry English-style mustard	10 mL
pinch	cayenne pepper	pinch
2 tbsp.	chopped fresh parsley	30 mL
1/2 cup	half-and-half cream or whipping cream	125 mL
4	hard-cooked eggs, chopped	4
	salt and pepper to taste	

Heat the oven to 325°F (160°C).

Place the fish in a large skillet and pour in enough water to just cover. Bring to a boil, cover, turn the heat to low and simmer 12-15 minutes, or until the fish flakes when tested with a fork. Lift the fish from the skillet with a slotted spoon, then skin, bone and flake fish. Cook the rice in boiling water 10 minutes or until cooked. Drain well. Steam the leeks about 5 minutes, until cooked.

Melt the butter in a medium saucepan. Remove it from the heat and add the turmeric, mustard, cayenne, parsley, cream and eggs. Stir in the fish, rice and leeks until the ingredients are well mixed. Season to taste with salt and pepper. Place in a buttered 2 quart (2 L) casserole. Cover with a lid or foil and bake about 20 minutes to heat through. Serve immediately, hot from the oven.

FRESH RED SNAPPER "VERACRUZ" STYLE

Travellers returning from Mexico bring back a fondness for fresh fish done "Veracruz" style—traditional red snapper with a zesty tomato sauce flavoured with onions, capers and sliced green olives. Serve with rice flavoured with bits of jalapeño peppers and fresh lime juice, hearty black beans, warm tortillas or corn bread, and a salad of romaine with thin slices of orange and avocado dressed in a herby vinaigrette. Serves 4.

1/3 cup	olive oil	75 mL
2 cups	onion, thinly sliced into strips	500 mL
1	*each* red and green bell pepper, halved, seeded, de-ribbed and cut into strips	1
3 1/2 cups	canned whole tomatoes, drained and coarsely diced	875 mL
1 tbsp.	*each* granulated sugar, sherry vinegar, and Spanish paprika	15 mL
4 tbsp.	capers, rinsed and drained	60 mL
2/3 cup	sliced pimiento-stuffed green olives	150 mL
1/2 tsp.	*each* salt and black pepper	2 mL
10 drops	liquid hot pepper (Tabasco) sauce	10 drops
2 lbs.	fresh red snapper fillets, rinsed and patted completely dry	1 kg
2 tbsp.	minced fresh parsley	30 mL

Prepare the sauce several hours ahead to allow time for the flavours to blend. Heat the olive oil in a large skillet over medium-high heat. Add the onion and peppers, and sauté the vegetables until softened and just golden. Add the tomatoes and cook over high heat until the sauce is thickened and bubbly and the juices are absorbed, about 7 minutes. Add the sugar, vinegar and paprika. Cook over medium heat for 5 minutes. Finally, add the capers, sliced olives, salt, pepper and hot pepper sauce. Heat for 5 minutes or until bubbly and set aside.

Heat the oven to 350°F (180°C). Brush olive oil on the bottom and sides of a 2-inch (5 cm) deep baking dish. Place the fish fillets in the dish. Spoon sauce over the fish and bake 30 minutes, or until the fish just flakes easily with a fork. Remove the dish from the oven and let it rest 10 minutes before serving. Sprinkle with minced parsley and serve at once.

# **G** OAN SPICED FRIED FISH

This recipe is named after Goa, a coastal region of India where fish dishes are popular. For this dish, Indian flavours spice up the subtle taste of fish, giving a colourful, tasty coating to cubes of red snapper or cod. Serve the fish with rice, green salad and chutney for an authentic eastern touch. Or serve it as appetizers on wooden cocktail sticks. Serves 4 as a main dish.

1 lb.	firm white fish (e.g. snapper or cod), skinned and boned	500 g
2 tsp.	curry powder	10 mL
1/2 tsp.	chili powder	2 mL
1 tsp.	ground coriander	5 mL
1 tsp.	ground turmeric	5 mL
1/2 tsp.	ground cumin	2 mL
1/2 tsp.	salt	2 mL
	vegetable oil, for frying	

Cut the fish into 2-inch (5 cm) cubes. On a large plate, combine the curry, chili, coriander, turmeric, cumin and salt. Toss the fish well in the spice mixture.

Pour enough oil into a medium heavy-based pan to come 1/2 inch (1 cm) up the sides. Heat the oil to 400°F (200°C). Lower the fish into the oil with a slotted spoon, half at a time, and fry over medium heat about 4 minutes or until it is dark golden and cooked in the centre. Lift it out with the slotted spoon onto paper towelling and keep it warm while frying the remaining fish. Serve immediately.

GRILLED SWORDFISH WITH LIME BUTTER

Thick, succulent fresh swordfish steaks are delicious grilled or broiled (or even pan-broiled in a sizzling hot skillet!) to a juicy turn, and topped with a generous dollop of chilled lime-flavoured butter. Serve with tiny steamed red-skinned potatoes, fresh field carrots, and a crisp romaine salad with slices of orange and purple onion. Offer a crisp, warm baguette to dip into the last of the delicious juices and lime butter. Serves 4.

1 1/4 cups	Lime Butter (recipe follows)	300 mL
4 tbsp.	olive oil	60 mL
2 tbsp.	fresh lime juice	30 mL
4	fresh swordfish steaks (about 2 lbs. (1 kg)), 3/4 inch (2 cm) thick	4
	salt and black pepper	

Prepare the Lime Butter and roll it into a log shape, 1 1/2 inches (4 cm) in diameter. Wrap it in waxed paper, seal, and chill several hours (or overnight) until firm.

Whisk together the olive oil and lime juice and brush both sides of the swordfish steaks with the mixture. Season the fish with salt and pepper, and let stand 20 minutes.

Lightly oil the broiler pan or grill. Broil or grill steaks 3 inches (7.5 cm) from the heat, turning once and cooking until slightly charred and a rich golden brown on each side. The finished fish steaks should *just* feel slightly firmed and opaque when done. Do not overcook.

Remove the fish from the heat, place it on warmed plates, and top each portion with a generous slice or two of chilled Lime Butter. Serve at once, sizzling hot.

LIME BUTTER
Makes 1 1/4 cups (300 mL).

1 cup	very fresh butter	250 mL
4 tbsp.	fresh lime juice	60 mL
2 tsp.	finely grated fresh lime peel	10 mL
1/2 tsp.	cracked black pepper	2 mL
3 tbsp.	finely minced fresh parsley	45 mL

Prepare the lime butter at least one day before using for the best flavour. Using a food processor, cream together the softened butter, lime juice, lime peel, pepper and parsley until thoroughly blended and fluffy. Store, chilled and sealed, until ready to use. Any leftover butter may be used to flavour broiled chicken, pork chops, or steamed vegetables.

STIR-FRY FISH PRIMAVERA

Use a firm-textured fish for this simple but elegant stir-fry: salmon, cod, halibut, shark and swordfish all work beautifully. Try different vegetables in the recipe, and serve it up with steaming nutty brown rice. Serves 1.

2 tbsp.	oil	30 mL
1	medium fish steak, cut into 1-inch (2.5 cm) cubes	1
1	green onion, sliced on the diagonal	1
	few slices of red onion	
	few slivers of red or green bell pepper	
1 tbsp.	soy sauce	15 mL
3-4	snow peas, slivered	3-4
	slivers of fresh oyster (or regular) mushrooms (optional)	
	salt and freshly ground black pepper to taste	
	cayenne pepper to taste	

Heat the oil in a wok or medium skillet over medium heat. Add the fish cubes and sear on all sides. Add the green onion, red onion and bell pepper along with the soy sauce and toss gently. Cover and cook for 2 minutes. Add the snow peas and mushrooms. Cover and cook for 1 minute. Taste for seasonings. Add the salt, pepper and/or cayenne to taste. Serve immediately.

S ALMON STEAKS WITH HOLLANDAISE SAUCE

All fish works well cooked in the microwave, and this recipe, calling for a simple, refreshing marinade and a feather-light Hollandaise, is a real winner. The sauce works just as well over a selection of microwave-steamed fresh vegetables. Serves 4.

4	salmon steaks, 1/2 inch (1 cm) thick	4
2/3 cup	dry white wine	150 mL
1 tbsp.	lemon juice	15 mL
1/2 tsp.	salt	2 mL
1/4 tsp.	white pepper	1 mL
3	egg whites, stiffly beaten	3
3	egg yolks, slightly beaten	3
1/2 cup	butter	125 mL
	lemon for garnish	

Vent the skin of each salmon steak along the backbone. Place the salmon in a shallow microproof dish.

Mix together the wine, lemon juice, salt and pepper. Pour it over the salmon, cover and refrigerate for 2 hours, turning the fish after 1 hour.

Drain the marinade from the salmon and reserve. Arrange the fish so that the thicker, denser parts are towards the outside edge of the dish. Cover with waxed paper and microwave on HIGH 100% power 7-9 minutes. Let stand, covered, while you make the Hollandaise sauce.

Place the butter in a 4-cup (1 L) microproof measure. Microwave on HIGH 100% power 30-60 seconds until melted. Blend in the reserved wine marinade. Microwave on HIGH 100% power 1 minute.

Blend about 1/2 cup (125 mL) of the wine/butter mixture into the egg yolks. Mix well and return to the remaining wine mixture in the measure. Blend well. Microwave on MEDIUM 50% power 1 minute, stir well and microwave on MEDIUM 50% power for a further 1 minute. Fold in the beaten egg whites.

Place the salmon steaks on a serving platter and top with Hollandaise Sauce. Garnish with lemon before serving.

.C. SALMON SOUFFLÉ

This impressive soufflé (they always are!) is a delicate luncheon or brunch dish, delicious with the first asparagus of the season, a tender bibb lettuce salad, and fresh baked dinner rolls. Use fresh salmon, poached or steamed—nothing can beat it. Serves 4.

3 tbsp.	*each* butter and all-purpose flour	45 mL
2 cups	milk	500 mL
4 tbsp.	*each* fresh snipped dill and chives	60 mL
1 tsp.	salt	5 mL
3	egg yolks	3
1/4 tsp.	white pepper	1 mL
2 cups	flaked cooked fresh salmon	500 mL
5	egg whites, at room temperature	5
	buttered fresh bread crumbs	

Heat the oven to 375°F (190°C). Butter the bottom and sides of a 6 cup (1.5 L) porcelain soufflé dish. Set aside.

Prepare the white sauce by melting the butter to foaming in a small saucepan over medium heat. Add the flour, all at once, and whisk 2-3 minutes until bubbly. Slowly add the milk, whisking constantly. Cook over medium heat to a medium-thick sauce. Remove the sauce from the heat. Whisk in the dill, chives, salt and pepper.

One at a time, beat in the egg yolks, mixing well. Gently fold in the flaked salmon. Beat the egg whites in a clean, grease-free bowl until stiff, but not dry. Fold in a third of the whites, to "loosen" the mixture. Very gently, scrape the remaining beaten whites into the mixture, and gently fold them in. Incorporate almost completely (some traces of white are fine), taking care not to deflate the soufflé mixture.

Pour the mixture into the prepared dish, making decorative deep swirls in the top with a blunt knife. Top with bread crumbs. Bake the soufflé 25-35 minutes, or until very puffy and high and golden brown on top.

Remove the soufflé from the oven, and serve it at once. To serve any soufflé properly, plunge two large dessert spoons straight down into the centre of the soufflé, and "pull" it into serving sections. The top will be drier and airier, and the centre should be moist (not runny). Each portion should have a bit of both.

BLACKENED SALMON FILLETS WITH FRESH CITRUS BUTTER

"Blackened" fish has gained popularity over the past few years, due primarily to Paul Prudhomme's method from the city of New Orleans. This version, less smoky and messy than the original, results in a superb fresh salmon — juicy and succulent on the inside, spicy and crusty on the outside. The melt of cooling fresh citrus-spiked butter is the perfect addition. Serve with Creole rice, fresh zucchini, and hot corn bread. Serves 4.

	Seasoning Mix (recipe follows)	
4	fresh salmon fillets, each about 6 oz. (180 g)	4
	oil	

Prepare the Seasoning Mix. Sprinkle it evenly on both sides of the salmon fillets, and allow to sit at room temperature for 20 minutes. Heat a cast-iron or heavy non-stick skillet over high heat. Brush the bottom of the skillet with oil to film. Sear the seasoned fillets quickly, 3 minutes, skin side first. Shake the skillet while the fillets are searing to prevent sticking. Using a flat metal spatula, flip the fillets, adding a new film of oil first. Sear the fillets 3-4 minutes. Fish is cooked when it just turns opaque, and is firm to the touch. Do not overcook.

Serve the blackened fillets on warmed plates, and top each at once with a pat or two of Fresh Citrus Butter. Serve hot.

FRESH CITRUS BUTTER

Use any leftover butter to top fresh vegetables, broiled chicken, or grilled burgers.

1 cup	butter, softened	250 mL
2 tbsp.	*each* fresh lime, orange and lemon juice	30 mL
1 tsp.	*each* finely grated lime, orange and lemon peel	5 mL
1/2 tsp.	white pepper	2 mL
15 drops	liquid hot pepper (Tabasco) sauce	15 drops
3 tbsp.	finely minced fresh parsley	45 mL

Prepare this butter at least one day before using for the best flavour. Using a food processor, cream together the butter, citrus juices, grated rinds, pepper, Tabasco and parsley until thoroughly blended and fluffy. Shape it into a roll 1 1/2 inches (3.5 cm) in diameter, and wrap it in waxed paper. Store, chilled, until ready to use.

SEASONING MIX

1 tsp.	*each* white pepper, black pepper, dried thyme, oregano, allspice, onion powder and garlic salt	5 mL
1 tbsp.	paprika	15 mL

Combine all ingredients thoroughly. Use the mix to season fresh fish fillets for "blackening".

Note: This recipe works well with fresh red snapper, roughy, swordfish and any other firm fish. Fish fillets should be 1/2 - 3/4 inch (1-2 cm) thick.

The Easy Gourmet features a photograph of this recipe on page 107.

TORTUNAS WITH MEXICAN SALSA

The flavours of Mexico inspired this easily-prepared supper dish. Flakes of tuna wrapped in tortillas give them a novel twist and the chile pepper gives a little heat to the salsa. (Beware of rubbing your face after handling the chile peppers, as they can cause irritation.) The salsa recipe can be halved for serving with the tortunas, or make the full amount and have some on hand to serve with corn chips. Serves 4.

SALSA:

5	medium tomatoes, peeled, seeded and chopped very fine	5
1	small red onion, peeled and chopped very fine	1
1	jalapeño chile pepper, seeded and chopped very fine	1
4 tbsp.	chopped fresh cilantro	60 mL
1/2 tsp.	salt	2 mL
2 tbsp.	fresh lime juice	30 mL
1 tsp.	olive oil	5 mL

Combine the tomatoes, onion, chile, cilantro, salt and lime juice in a medium bowl. (Or process these ingredients in a food processor until finely chopped.) Cover and leave to marinate 1 hour. Before serving, pour off any water that may have separated out, then stir in the olive oil. Makes 2 cups (500 mL).

TORTILLA FILLING:

2	ripe avocados, peeled and seeded	2
1/2 cup	cream cheese, at room temperature	125 mL
1 cup	sour cream	250 mL
1	clove garlic, crushed	1
1/2 tsp.	chili powder	2 mL
1/2 tsp.	lemon juice	2 mL
8	flour tortillas, about 8 inches (20 cm) round	8
1	6 1/2 oz. (184 g) can tuna, drained and flaked	1
	black pepper	
1 cup	grated Mozzarella cheese	250 mL
2	green onions, chopped	2

Heat the oven to 350°F (180°C). Mash the avocados with a fork in a medium bowl and beat in the cream cheese, sour cream, garlic, chili powder and lemon juice. Lay the tortillas on a working surface and divide the avocado mixture among them, in a line down the centre of each one. Top each with some of the tuna and sprinkle with black pepper. Roll up the tortillas and place them seam side down in a single layer in a shallow buttered 10 x 10 inch (25 x 25 cm) ovenproof dish. Sprinkle the cheese and green onions over top. Bake, covered, until the tortunas are heated through and the cheese has melted, about 25 minutes. Serve with salsa.

WEST COAST SHELLFISH CIOPPINO

This San Francisco-inspired seafood stew is loaded with choice shellfish swathed in a wonderful red sauce of tomatoes, garlic and peppers. Created by the Italian docksmen on the famed Fisherman's Wharf, this dish needs only a great loaf of fresh sourdough bread, cut into thick wedges, to complete the meal. Serves 6-8.

1/2 cup	olive oil	125 mL
2 cups	onion, sliced into slivers (about 2 medium onions)	500 mL
2	large cloves garlic, slivered	2
4	stalks celery, sliced	4
1	large green bell pepper, de-ribbed, seeded and sliced into slivers	1
1/2 lb.	fresh mushrooms, wiped clean and sliced	125 g
1 tbsp.	*each* sugar and red wine vinegar	15 mL
4 cups	coarsely chopped tomatoes (canned or fresh), about 5 medium tomatoes	1 L
1	14 oz. (398 mL) can tomato pureé	1
1 cup	red wine	250 mL
1 tsp.	dried red pepper flakes	5 mL
1 tsp.	liquid hot pepper (Tabasco) sauce, or to taste	5 mL
1 lb.	prawns or large shrimp, shelled and deveined, tails intact	500 g
1 lb.	swordfish, cut into 1 inch (2.5 cm) cubes	500 g
1 lb.	fresh mussels, scrubbed and steamed open	500 g
1 lb.	fresh clams, scrubbed and steamed open	500 g
1	large Dungeness crab, about 2 lbs (1 kg), cooked, chilled and cut up in large pieces; or 1 lb. (500 g) imitation crab meat	1
1/3 cup	minced fresh parsley	75 mL
	salt and cracked black pepper	

Heat the olive oil in a very deep stock pot over medium-high heat. Add the onion, garlic, celery and green peppers, and sauté, stirring, for 5-7 minutes until the vegetables are softened and pale golden in colour. Add the mushrooms, and sauté 5 minutes. Stir in the sugar and vinegar, add the tomatoes, tomato pureé, wine, red pepper flakes, and Tabasco. Bring the mixture to a gentle boil, reduce to a simmer, and cook about 1 hour, partially covered, to blend the flavours.

Uncover the pot, and add the prawns and swordfish. Cook over medium heat about 5-6 minutes. Break off and discard the empty half-shell of each mussel and clam, and add the meaty half-shells to the pot. Add the crab meat. Heat the cioppino over medium-low heat for 15 minutes until heated through and piping hot. Taste and correct the seasonings with salt and pepper. Stir in the minced parsley, and serve at once. Provide lots of fresh sourdough bread for dunking, and bowls for the empty shells. Large napkins are in order for this meal!

The Easy Gourmet features a photograph of this recipe on page 125.

GOLDMINER OYSTER "HANGTOWN FRY"

In California's early gold-rush days, a condemned man was granted the request of his last meal. He chose the three (then) most expensive ingredients he could think of: oysters, eggs, and bacon. This version of that original dish uses Canada's wonderful east and west coast oysters. Garnish the dish with watercress, and pass the buttermilk biscuits and hot coffee. Serves 4.

8	slices bacon	8
5 tbsp.	butter	75 mL
1	*each* green and red bell pepper, diced	1
1/2 cup	thinly sliced green onions	125 mL
	hot pepper (Tabasco) sauce to taste	
12	shucked oysters, patted dry	12
1 cup	corn flour (finely ground corn meal)	250 mL
	or all-purpose flour	
2 tbsp.	vegetable oil	30 mL
8	eggs	8
1 tsp.	salt	2 mL
1/2 tsp.	cracked black pepper	1 mL
1/3 cup	cream	75 mL
3 tbsp.	finely minced fresh parsley	45 mL

In a large skillet, fry the bacon until crisp. Lift the bacon from the skillet. Keep it warm, and reserve the drippings. Heat 2 tbsp. (30 mL) of the butter in a skillet, add the diced pepper and green onions, and sauté until they are softened and the edges begin to colour. Season with Tabasco. Set aside.

Dredge the oysters lightly with flour (corn flour makes it crispier), shaking off the excess. Add the oil to the bacon drippings, and heat over medium-high heat 3-4 minutes. Fry the oysters quickly, 1-2 minutes per side, in the hot fat until crispy and golden brown. Add the hot oysters to the vegetables.

Beat the eggs with the salt, pepper, and cream. Heat the remaining 3 tbsp. (45 mL) butter in a skillet until foaming. Add the eggs to the hot skillet, and quickly scramble the eggs just until set (do not cook dry).

To serve, mound the scrambled eggs on a warmed platter. Top with the vegetables and fried oysters. Garnish with the crisp bacon, sprinkle the works with parsley, and serve at once—piping hot.

USSELS MARINARA

Sweet and succulent, mussels prepared this way are one of the best loved treats in the coastal towns on the French and Spanish Riviera, as well as our own east and west coasts. Don't forget to serve a fresh loaf of chewy bread — you won't want to waste a drop of the fragrant juices. Serves 4.

4 tbsp.	oil	60 mL
1	small onion, finely chopped	1
1	clove garlic, finely chopped	1
1	14 oz. (398 mL) can tomatoes, drained	1
	salt, pepper and cayenne to taste	
1/2 cup	dry white wine, chicken stock or canned broth	125 mL
1/2 cup	water	125 mL
1	small onion, sliced	1
1	bay leaf	1
2 lbs.	mussels, well rinsed	1 kg
	parsley for garnish	

Heat the oil in a medium saucepan. Add the chopped onion and sauté gently until soft. Add the garlic and cook another minute or so. Add the tomatoes, breaking them up with a spoon. Cover and simmer for 10 minutes. Season to taste with salt, pepper and cayenne.

In a large saucepan bring the wine and water to a boil. Add the sliced onion, garlic, bay leaf and mussels. Cover and steam until the mussels pop open, about 5 minutes. Remove from heat. Discard the liquid and any mussels that did not open.

Place the mussels on a serving plate and spoon tomato sauce over them. Garnish with whole or chopped parsley.

BEER STEAMED CLAMS WITH DEVILED DIPPING SAUCE

Buy a load of fresh clams in the shell, steam 'em open in beer, and have a feast. Nothing could be simpler, or more fun. Provide a bucket for the empty shells, some big napkins, and lots of hot french fries or big, thick potato chips. In the summer, partner the clams with fresh corn-on-the-cob. Serves 4-6.

Deviled Dipping Sauce:

2 cups	mayonnaise	500 mL
1 tsp.	dry mustard	5 mL
pinch	cayenne pepper	pinch
1 tsp.	liquid hot pepper (Tabasco) sauce	5 mL
2 tbsp.	Dijon-style mustard	30 mL
1 tsp.	brown sugar	5 mL
1 tsp.	cider vinegar	5 mL
6 dozen	fresh clams in their shells (Littleneck variety are excellent), scrubbed	6 dozen
2	12 oz. (341 mL) bottles of beer or non-alcoholic beer	2

Prepare the sauce several hours before serving. Combine the mayonnaise, dry mustard, cayenne, Tabasco, Dijon-style mustard, brown sugar and vinegar. Whisk until smooth and thoroughly combined. Chill, covered, before serving for the best flavour.

Place the scrubbed clams in a large, deep pot, pour the beer over top, and bring to a simmer over medium heat. Cover, and steam the clams 5-7 minutes or until they are completely open. Discard any clams that refuse to open. Serve the clams in deep, wide, warmed bowls, and provide long forks for dipping the succulent clam meat into the dipping sauce.

Opposite: West Coast Shellfish Cioppino (page 120).

CRISPY CLAM FRITTERS

Who doesn't like something crispy and fried to munch! And these golden brown clam fritters always fill the bill. They make a great supper along with a bowl of homemade cole slaw or potato salad, fresh cherry tomatoes, and crisp raw vegetables. And nothing can beat them as a mouth-watering appetizer. Either way, enjoyment is a sure bet. Serves 6 (makes 24-32 fritters).

1 3/4 cups	shucked baby clams, drained	425 mL
1 tsp.	all-purpose flour	5 mL
1 tsp.	salt	5 mL
1 tbsp.	paprika	15 mL
1/2 tsp.	baking powder	2 mL
1/4 tsp.	sugar	1 mL
1 tsp.	*each* ground allspice and nutmeg	2 mL
	cracked black pepper	
2	eggs, lightly beaten	2
1/3 cup	finely minced green onions	75 mL
3 tbsp.	finely minced fresh parsley	45 mL
1/2 cup	whipping cream	125 mL
1/2 cup	half-and-half cream	125 mL
2 tbsp.	melted butter	30 mL
2 cups	vegetable or corn oil for frying	500 mL
	lemon wedges	

Sift together the flour, salt, paprika, baking powder, sugar, allspice, nutmeg and black pepper. Beat together the eggs, green onions, parsley, cream, melted butter and clams. Make a well in the centre of the dry ingredients, and stir in the liquid mixture.

Heat the oil in a large, deep skillet to a depth of 2 inches (5 cm). Heat to 375°F (190°C) (test by dropping a bit of batter into the oil; it should sizzle at once and float right up to the top). Drop the fritter batter by tablespoons into the hot oil, and fry until crispy and golden brown on both sides, about 3-4 minutes. Do not crowd the fritters, or they will "steam" rather than fry up crispy.

Drain the fritters on absorbent paper, salt lightly while hot, and serve at once.

SOUTHERN-STYLE CREAMY CORN AND CLAM CHOWDER

Thick stick-to-the-ribs hearty corn and clam chowder is wonderful as the "main event" on a wintery evening. Ladle it up, steaming hot, into wide soup bowls. Top with crispy crumbled bacon, sliced green onions, and a generous twist of the pepper grinder—and dig in! Add a basket of hot homemade biscuits and a crock of butter. Serves 8.

2 oz.	lean salt pork, diced (or 3 slices bacon)	60 g
4 tbsp.	unsalted butter	60 mL
2 cups	chopped onion	500 mL
1 cup	chopped celery	250 mL
1	large green pepper, diced	1
8	medium-sized potatoes, peeled and diced	8
4 cups	half-and-half cream	1 L
4 cups	milk	1 L
5 cups	whole kernel corn (if using frozen, thaw, cook 3 minutes and drain)	1.25 L
1/2 tsp.	*each* dried thyme, nutmeg and black pepper	2 mL
2 cups	shucked fresh baby clams	500 mL
2 oz.	diced red pimiento	60 g
	salt to taste	
8	slices bacon, fried crisp and crumbled	8
	thinly sliced green onions	
1/2 cup	milk or clam juice ("clam liqueur") as needed to thin chowder	125 mL

Sauté the salt pork in a large, deep stock pot over medium heat until softened and just golden. Add the butter, heat to bubbly, and stir in the onions, celery and green pepper. Sauté over medium-high heat until softened and pale golden in colour, about 10-12 minutes. Meanwhile, cook the diced potatoes in boiling, salted water 5-6 minutes until just tender. Drain completely.

Add the cream and milk to the vegetable mixture. Heat over low heat until simmering hot. Add the potatoes, corn, thyme, nutmeg and black pepper. Simmer 10 minutes. Finally, add the shucked clams and pimiento and cook the chowder over low heat just until clams are tender, 5-6 minutes. Remove the chowder from the heat, and allow it to stand 1-3 hours for the flavours to blend, and for the soup to thicken.

Gently reheat the chowder before serving, thinning as necessary to the desired consistency with milk or clam juice and adding salt to taste. Serve piping hot with crumbled bacon and sliced green onions on each serving. Pass the pepper grinder!

SCALLOPS IN LEMON SAUCE

Delicately seasoned with herbs, this dish is so sophisticated no one would guess how easy it is to prepare, and it works equally well as appetizer or entrée. Buttered, steamed rice and a big bright green salad complete the dinner. Serves 4.

4 tbsp.	butter	60 mL
2 tbsp.	finely chopped green onions	30 mL
4 tbsp.	finely chopped mushrooms	60 mL
2 tbsp.	lemon juice	30 mL
1 tbsp.	finely grated lemon rind	15 mL
1 tsp.	Worcestershire sauce	5 mL
1/2 tsp.	seasoned salt	2 mL
1/2 tsp.	dried tarragon	2 mL
1/4 tsp.	dried chervil	1 mL
1 cup	whipping cream	250 mL
1 lb.	scallops	500 g
	chopped parsley and lemon wedges for garnish	

Place the butter, green onions and mushrooms in a 6-cup (1.5 L) microproof dish. Cover and microwave on HIGH 100% power 2-4 minutes until the vegetables are softened, stirring once during cooking time.

Blend in the lemon juice, lemon rind, Worcestershire sauce, salt and herbs. Cover and microwave on MEDIUM 50% power 5 minutes, stirring once during cooking time.

Stir in the cream, return to the microwave and cook, uncovered, on MEDIUM 50% power 2-4 minutes until the cream is heated through (do not allow to boil).

Stir in the scallops and microwave, uncovered, on MEDIUM 50% power 3-5 minutes until the scallops are heated through.

Serve garnished with chopped parsley and lemon wedges.

BACON-WRAPPED SCALLOP BROCHETTES

These simply grilled fresh scallop brochettes are a savoury solution to a quick supper. Wrapped in bacon and threaded on skewers with bright cherry tomatoes and slivers of onion, these wonderful brochettes need only a wedge of lemon and a dollop of chilled tartar sauce. Serve with nutty brown rice and stir-fried vegetables. Serves 4.

8	slices bacon, cut into 1 inch (2.5 cm) pieces	8
1	large onion, cut into 1 inch (2.5 cm) chunks, separated into single layers	1
1 1/2 lbs.	fresh large scallops, 1 1/2 inch (3.5 cm) in diameter	750 g
16	cherry tomatoes, rinsed	16
1/3 cup	peanut oil	75 mL
2 tbsp.	soy sauce	30 mL
1 tbsp.	*each* brown sugar and cider vinegar	15 mL
1 tbsp.	finely grated fresh ginger	15 mL
	lemon wedges	
	tartar sauce	

Bring a small saucepan of water to a simmer, and blanch the bacon slices for 3 minutes. Remove them with a slotted spoon and drain on absorbent paper. Drop the onion into the water and blanch 2 minutes to soften slightly. Drain and pat dry.

Thread the scallops onto skewers (if you are using bamboo skewers, soak them in warm water 25 minutes before using to prevent burning), alternating with pieces of bacon, onion, and cherry tomatoes. Lay the filled skewers on a flat baking sheet. Whisk together the oil, soy sauce, brown sugar, cider vinegar and ginger until smooth. Brush the marinade over the filled skewers, and allow them to sit 25 minutes before grilling.

Heat the broiler or barbecue coals. Broil the brochettes 4 inches (10 cm) from the heat source for 6-8 minutes, turning once or twice and brushing with marinade several times. Grill only until the edges of the scallops are charred, the flesh is opaque, and the scallops feel slightly firm when pressed. Do not overcook. Remove the brochettes from the heat. Serve accompanied by lemon wedges and a bowl of chilled tartar sauce.

QUICK CRAB BISQUE

Microwave cooking and convenience foods make this bisque as quick as it is elegant, whether you serve it as an inviting first course at dinner, or accompany it with toasted cheese sticks for a perfect light lunch. Serves 4.

1/4 lb.	imitation crab meat, very finely flaked	125 g
1/3 cup	dry sherry	75 mL
1	10 oz. (284 mL) can tomato soup	1
5 oz.	tomato juice	150 mL
1 cup	half-and-half cream	250 mL
4	thin slices of lemon	4

Soak the crab in the sherry for about 1 hour.

In a microproof dish, combine the tomato soup and juice. Microwave on HIGH 100% power 2-4 minutes to bring to a boil, stirring once during cooking time. Let stand for about 2 minutes to cool slightly. Stir in the cream and sherry-soaked crab, reserving a few pieces of the crab for garnish.

Return to the microwave and cook on MEDIUM 50% power 2-4 minutes until heated through, stirring once during cooking time. Do not allow to boil—reduce power level further if necessary.

Serve garnished with lemon slices and the reserved flaked crab.

The Easy Gourmet features a photograph of this recipe on page 107.

T SAWWASSEN BEACH CRAB AU GRATIN

This creamy company casserole, with its rich bechamel sauce and the indescribable flavour of crab, is wonderful after a bracing winter walk on the beach. Serve it with a crunchy, colourful vegetable salad and hot drinks. Makes four 1 cup (250 mL) portions.

8 oz.	fresh crab meat (or imitation crab meat)	250 g
2 cups	cooked long-grain rice	500 mL
1 cup	grated Cheddar cheese	250 mL
2	hard-cooked eggs, sliced	2
1/2 cup	sliced or chopped green bell pepper	125 mL
2 tbsp.	butter	30 mL

Sauce:

1 1/2 tbsp.	butter	25 mL
1 1/2 tbsp.	all-purpose flour	25 mL
1 1/2 cups	milk	375 mL
3 tbsp.	mayonnaise	45 mL
	salt and pepper to taste	
1 cup	finely cubed bread	250 mL
	butter	

Heat the oven to 350°F (180°C). Grease a 2 quart (2 L) shallow casserole. Check the crab over and discard any shell. Place the rice in the casserole. Distribute the crab over top. Sprinkle with the cheese and the sliced eggs. Cook the green pepper in the butter until soft and layer on top of the eggs.

To make the sauce, melt the butter in a small saucepan. Stir in the flour to make a thick roux. Whisk in the milk and stir until smooth. Remove from the heat and add the mayonnaise. Season to taste with salt and pepper. Pour the sauce over the casserole ingredients.

Melt a little butter in a skillet and toss in the bread cubes. Stir to coat and sprinkle over the casserole. Cover and bake until heated through and bubbling, 30-40 minutes. Remove the cover and bake a further 5-10 minutes or until the bread cubes are crisped and browned.

CAJUN CRABCAKES

Flavourful crab pressed into cakes with onion and hot pepper sauce, browned southern-style in hot shortening—a winner every time, whether you make tiny cakes for hors d'oeuvres or larger ones for lunch. As a main dish, the crabcakes are beautifully set off by a salad of romaine and cherry tomatoes with citrus vinaigrette. Make sure to mash the potatoes by hand so they will be perfect for binding the cakes together. Makes ten 2-inch (5 cm) cakes.

1 lb.	fresh or imitation crab meat	500 g
1	small onion, peeled and halved	1
1	strip green bell pepper, about 1 inch (2.5 cm) wide	1
1 3/4 cup	unseasoned, cooled mashed potatoes, firmly packed (about 3 medium)	425 mL
2	eggs, lightly beaten	2
dash	freshly ground black pepper	dash
	hot pepper (Tabasco) sauce, to taste	
1/2 cup	fine dry bread crumbs or corn meal for dredging	125 mL
4 tbsp.	solid vegetable shortening	60 mL

In a food processor or blender, mince the crab meat, one-third at a time, emptying each third into a large bowl as it is done. Without cleaning the work bowl, mince the onion and pepper. Add to the crab along with the mashed potatoes, eggs, pepper and hot pepper sauce. Mix thoroughly with your hands, then shape into flat patties about 1/2 inch (1 cm) thick and 1 inch (2.5 cm) in diameter for small cakes, 2 inches (5 cm) in diameter for larger ones. Dredge the patties in the crumbs (or corn meal). Place them on a baking sheet lined with waxed paper, cover loosely and chill several hours before cooking to allow the patties to firm up.

Heat the shortening in a large heavy skillet over medium heat until sizzling hot, then brown the cakes well on both sides, about 3-5 minutes. Drain on paper towelling and serve immediately.

CREOLE BBQ SHRIMP, CAJUN-STYLE

Anyone who has ever visited that "eating town" of all towns—New Orleans— has had the local version of barbecued shrimp. Not really barbecued at all, but done up in a buttery, spicy sauce, this is a messy, fun, delicious dish to share with friends. Provide bowls for the shells, big cloth napkins, and lots of warmed sourdough bread for dunking into the fabulous sauce. Serves 4, or 6-8 as an appetizer.

2 lbs.	very large whole shrimp or prawns, shells on; fresh and uncooked	1 kg
1 cup	butter	250 mL
1 cup	olive oil	250 mL
3	large cloves garlic, minced	3
3	bay leaves, crumbled	3
1 tsp.	*each* dried oregano, basil, rosemary, thyme, salt, black pepper and cayenne	5 mL
1 tbsp.	pepper	15 mL
12 drops	paprika	12 drops
2 tbsp.	liquid hot pepper (Tabasco) sauce	30 mL
	fresh lemon juice	
	grated rind of 1 lemon	

Slit the underside of each shrimp halfway through, lengthwise, leaving the shell intact. Gently pull off the legs and discard.

In a large, heavy skillet, heat the butter until melted. Whisk in the oil, garlic, bay leaves, oregano, basil, rosemary, thyme, salt, pepper, cayenne, paprika, Tabasco, lemon juice and rind. Heat the sauce to a simmer, and simmer 15 minutes. Remove the sauce from the heat, and set aside for 45 minutes. Heat the oven to 375°F (190°C).

Reheat the sauce to bubbling, and add shrimp. Cook 1 minute, place the pan in the hot oven, and cook 10-12 minutes or until shrimp turn pink or red. Do not overcook.

Divide the shrimp among 4 wide, shallow bowls. Ladle sauce over each, and serve at once. Knives and forks work well, but fingers are the most fun.
The Easy Gourmet features a photograph of this recipe on the front cover.

W RAPAROUND PRAWNS ON SWEET AND SOUR SAUCE

Succulent prawns served on a colourful bed of sweet-and-sour sauce will get any dinner party off to a good start. Or make this a dual-purpose recipe and serve the prawns on rice as a main meal for three or four. Makes 6-8 appetizer servings.

1 lb.	fresh Tiger Bay prawns, in the shell	500 g
8-10	strips bacon	8-10

Sweet and Sour Sauce:

2 tbsp.	vegetable oil	30 mL
1	small onion, chopped very fine	1
1	clove garlic, crushed	1
1	medium tomato, skinned and diced	1
1	small green bell pepper, cored, seeded and diced	1
4 tsp.	sugar	20 mL
1 tbsp.	tomato paste	15 mL
1 tbsp.	soy sauce	15 mL
2/3 cup	chicken stock or bouillon	150 mL
1 tbsp.	fresh lime juice	15 mL
1 tbsp.	Chinese cooking wine (optional)	15 mL
1/2 cup	drained pineapple tidbits, chopped	125 mL
2 tsp.	cornstarch	10 mL
2 tsp.	water	10 mL
	chopped cilantro for garnish	

Shell the prawns, leaving the tails on. Remove the centre black veins. Cut each bacon strip into thirds and wrap one piece around each prawn. Secure each with a wooden cocktail stick. Place the prawns seam side down, in a single layer on a foil-lined jelly roll pan. Set aside in the refrigerator until ready to cook.

To make the sauce, heat the oil in a skillet over medium heat and sauté the onion and garlic until the onion is soft but not brown. Stir in the tomato, green bell pepper, sugar, tomato paste, soy sauce, stock, lime juice and cooking wine. Bring to a boil, stirring. Reduce the heat to low, add the pineapple and simmer 3-4 minutes. Combine the cornstarch with the water and stir it into sauce until thickened. Keep warm over low heat.

REAMY SHRIMP WITH PASTA

Pick up fresh pasta and shrimp on your way home from work, toss a salad and warm up some buns. Dinner will be ready in the time it takes you to boil a pot of water for the pasta! Serves 2-3 as a main course, 4-5 as a first course.

2 cups	whipping cream	500 mL
1 lb.	fresh pasta (fettuccine or linguine)	500 g
1 lb.	fresh cooked shrimp	500 g
	freshly ground black pepper	
	fresh herbs such as parsley, chives, oregano or basil for garnish	

Fill a large pot with water and bring it to a boil. Meanwhile, in a medium to large skillet, bring the whipping cream to a boil, reduce the heat to medium and boil until slightly thickened, about 5 minutes.

Add the pasta to the pot of boiling water and cook *al dente* (just firm to the bite), about 5 minutes.

Add the shrimp to the thickened cream and toss and turn it to heat and coat the shrimp with sauce. Taste for seasonings and add pepper and fresh herbs as necessary. Drain the pasta and place it on serving dishes. Spoon on the shrimp mixture, garnish with a few leaves of fresh herbs, and serve immediately.

HRIMP STUFFED SOLE WITH AURORA SAUCE

Serve this pretty dish—brimming with taste of the seashore—as an elegant luncheon or light supper, served on your most delicate china. Each serving is topped with the rich Aurora Sauce—a velouté sauce with tomato. Serve the sole with fresh seasonal asparagus spears, steamed rice, and a few cherry tomatoes for colour. Serves 6.

2 tbsp.	butter	30 mL
1/2 cup	finely crushed cracker crumbs	125 mL
1 tsp.	finely chopped fresh herbs—parsley, tarragon, or basil	5 mL
6 oz.	fresh shrimp	180 g
3	whole sole fillets, halved lengthwise	3
	Aurora Sauce (recipe follows)	

Melt the butter 30-40 seconds in a microproof bowl. Blend in the cracker crumbs, herbs and shrimp. Divide the mixture evenly among the sole fillets, spreading the filling over the skin side of the fish.

Roll the fillets and secure each with a toothpick. Arrange them in a circle on a microproof plate. The fish may be covered and refrigerated at this point.

To cook the fish, cover with waxed paper and microwave on HIGH 100% power 3-4 minutes until the sole is cooked. Reheat the Aurora Sauce on MEDIUM 50% power, stirring once or twice during cooking time.

To serve, place a little of the sauce on a serving plate. Remove the toothpicks from the fish and place the fish on top of the sauce. Garnish with a few sprigs of fresh herbs.

AURORA SAUCE:

2 tbsp.	all-purpose flour	30 mL
2 tbsp.	butter	30 mL
1 cup	fish stock	250 mL
1/2 tsp.	salt	2 mL
1/4 tsp.	white pepper	1 mL
2 tbsp.	whipping cream	30 mL
2 tbsp.	tomato paste	30 mL

Place the flour and butter in a microproof 4-cup (1 L) measure. Microwave on HIGH 100% power 30-50 seconds until the butter is melted. Stir well and gradually blend in the fish stock, salt and pepper. Return to the microwave and cook on HIGH 100% power 2 minutes, stir well and microwave for a further 2 minutes until the mixture comes to a boil. Stir and blend in the cream and tomato paste. Adjust seasonings if necessary. The sauce may be covered and refrigerated at this point.

TROUT AMANDINE

Beautiful to look at and delicately flavoured, trout is a versatile and nutritious main dish. Small brook trout are usually 8-12 inches (20-30 cm) long and can be served whole—just wash and clean them. Serve one whole trout to each guest, or two or three if they are quite small. Trout as the main course calls for pan-fried potatoes, broiled squash or zucchini, and lots of lemons. Serves 4.

4	trout	4
6 tbsp.	butter	90 mL
	all-purpose flour for dredging	
1 cup	whole blanched almonds	250 mL
	freshly ground black pepper	
	parsley for garnish	

Melt the butter over medium-high heat in a large skillet or two medium pans (or fry the fish, one at a time, in a smaller pan). When the butter is melted and bubbling, dip the fish in the flour and place in the hot butter. Add the almonds and stir to brown the nuts evenly. Fry the fish for 10 minutes per inch (2.5 cm) of thickness measured at the thickest part, turning after 5 minutes. They should be crisp and golden looking. Season to taste with pepper, spoon over the toasted nuts and sprinkle with parsley. Serve immediately.

TROUT SMOTHERED IN MUSHROOMS

This recipe for gorgeous fresh trout is a snap to prepare, with total time needed under 1 hour. The finished results are impressive—the trout served under a blanket of rich and creamy mushroom sauce flavoured with a hint of garlic. Ideal accompaniments are parsley-buttered tiny nugget potatoes, stir-fried fresh carrots and broccoli, and tiny hot dinner rolls. Serves 4.

4	trout	4
1/2 lb.	fresh mushrooms	250 g
4 tbsp.	butter	60 mL
1	clove garlic, minced	1
1 cup + 2 tbsp	whipping cream	280 mL
	freshly ground black pepper	

Wash the trout and pat it dry. Sauté the mushrooms in butter until soft. Add the garlic and cook for a few seconds. Add 2 tbsp. (30 mL) of the cream and let the sauce boil until slightly thickened, about 4 minutes.

Heat the oven to 425°F (220°C). Grease a baking dish that will hold the fish in one layer. Place the fish in the dish and pour the mushroom sauce over it. Bake 10 minutes per inch (2.5 cm) of thickness measured at the thickest part. Lift the trout onto a hot platter. Pour the pan juices into a small saucepan and add the remaining 1 cup (250 mL) of cream. Bring to a boil and boil until reduced by half and thickened, about 5 minutes. Season to taste and pour the sauce over the trout. Serve immediately.

EGGS AND CHEESE

Easy on the budget, light and nourishing, protein-packed, Safeway's fresh eggs and cheeses from around the world can always be kept on hand for everything from Scrambled Eggs Royale or Canadian White Cheddar Rarebit to more adventurous fare—Blue Cheese, Leek and Nut Quiche or Eggs Benedict "Fruits de Mer."

S AVOURY SCRAMBLED EGGS IN A PITA POCKET

Here is a quick, convenient, and fun variation on a classic breakfast or brunch dish—all the goodness of eggs, dressed up with ham and tomatoes and tucked into pita bread. Serves 2.

1/2	small onion, finely chopped	1/2
2 tbsp.	butter	30 mL
2	medium tomatoes, coarsely chopped	2
	few slices of ham or spicy sausage, diced	
4	large eggs, lightly beaten	4
dash	hot pepper (Tabasco) sauce	dash
	salt and pepper to taste	
2 tbsp.	herbs such as parsley, chives or basil	30 mL
	pita bread	

Over medium heat, sauté the onion in the butter until soft. Add the tomatoes and ham and cook for another 2-3 minutes. Stir in the eggs and season to taste. Stir in the herbs. Continue cooking, stirring occasionally, until the eggs are just set, about 2 minutes more.

Cut the pita bread into halves and fill the pockets with the egg mixture. Serve at once.

Opposite: Blue Cheese Leek and Nut Quiche (page 155), Make-Ahead Eggs Benedict (page 145), Eggs Benedict "Fruits de Mer" (page 146), and Scrambled Eggs Royale (page 148).

AKE-AHEAD EGGS BENEDICT

The mad rush of making Eggs Benedict is over forever! Poach the eggs in advance and make the Hollandaise the easy blender way, and everything will be ready at the right moment. Serve with a couple of spears of fresh steamed asparagus, toasted English muffin halves, and an extra dollop (or two) of Hollandaise. Serves 4.

4	large eggs	4
4	English muffins, split	4
4	thin slices of Black Forest ham	4
	Hollandaise The Easy Way (recipe follows)	

Bring a large pot of water to a boil and reduce the heat to a gentle simmer. One at a time, break the eggs and slip them into the water. Cook the eggs for 3 minutes and remove them into ice water. To reheat, immerse in almost simmering water for 1-2 minutes. Eggs may be kept in this manner for up to 2 days, refrigerated.

Just before serving time, toast the muffins and top one half of each with a slice of ham. While the eggs are reheating, make the Hollandaise Sauce. Place an egg on the ham, pour a little sauce over the top and serve immediately.

HOLLANDAISE THE EASY WAY

Make this sauce just before serving—the fresher the better.

3	egg yolks	3
2 tbsp.	lemon juice	30 mL
pinch	cayenne pepper	pinch
dash	salt	dash
	freshly ground black pepper	
1/2 cup	butter, melted and bubbling hot	125 mL

Mix together in a blender the egg yolks, lemon juice and seasonings. With the machine running, very slowly pour in the butter. Run the machine a little longer until the sauce thickens. Spoon it over the eggs, and serve any extra sauce in a pretty dish at the table.

The Easy Gourmet features a photograph of this recipe on page 143.

E GGS BENEDICT "FRUITS DE MER" WITH CITRUS HOLLANDAISE

This version of everyone's favourite brunch dish features the familiar poached eggs topped with crab meat and shrimp, all topped with a tangy citrus-spiked Hollandaise sauce. Serve over toasted English muffins or crumpets, garnish with crisp watercress and thin twists of fresh lemon and orange, and serve piping hot. Truly a royal breakfast dish! Serves 4.

4	English muffins, split *or*	4
8	crumpets	8
8	eggs, poached and kept warm	8
6 oz.	crab meat (fresh or canned) or imitation crab meat, roughly flaked	185 g
6 oz.	cooked and chilled tiny shrimp	185 g
	Citrus Hollandaise (recipe follows)	
	pinch paprika or cracked black pepper	
	watercress and twists of orange and lemon for garnish	

Lightly toast the English muffins (or crumpets) and keep warm. Poach the eggs, and keep warm in a crockery bowl of tepid water (this trick is great when entertaining, and avoids the last-minute hassle of poaching the eggs). Have ready the flaked crab meat and cooked shrimp.

Prepare the sauce, and keep it warm no longer than 20 minutes over (not touching) barely simmering water.

On each plate, place 2 muffin halves (or 2 crumpets). Combine the flaked crab meat and shrimp, divide into 8 portions, and place it on top of the muffins. Top each with a warm poached egg. Top each egg with a generous spoonful of hot Hollandaise sauce. Add a pinch of paprika or cracked pepper to the top of each serving, garnish with crisp watercress, and tuck in twists of thin citrus slices. Serve at once.

The Easy Gourmet features a photograph of this recipe on page 143.

CITRUS HOLLANDAISE

Makes 1 1/2 cups (375 mL).

3	egg yolks, at room temperature	3
2 tbsp.	*each* fresh orange and lemon juice	30 mL
1/4 tsp.	salt	1 mL
1 cup	unsalted butter, melted	250 mL

In the top of a double boiler, whisk together the egg yolks, 1 tbsp. (15 mL) each of the orange and lemon juice, and the salt until thick and very creamy. Place the pan over simmering water and continue to whisk the mixture until just thickened (the mixture will begin to leave "tracks" as you whisk).

Remove the pan from the heat, and in a very slow, steady stream, begin to whisk in the butter. Add the butter slowly, making sure that the egg yolks absorb the butter you have added before adding more. Finally, whisk in the remaining orange and lemon juice. Whisk completely smooth. Serve warm.

Note: Substituting the popular imitation crab meat found in the fresh fish department will lower considerably the cholesterol level in this dish. Packaged dry Hollandaise mixes, prepared according to directions, are convenient when speed is of the essence. Liven them up a bit by adding the fresh orange and lemon juice, and a pinch of dry or prepared mustard.

CRAMBLED EGGS ROYALE

The ultimate in scrambled eggs! Served for brunch, or as a party appetizer, this dressed-up classic is fit for a king. Substitute cottage cheese for the butter, and you have a delicious variation on a great recipe. A generous bowl of fresh fruit salad or orange sections and cool melon slices is the perfect complement. Serves 4.

4 tbsp.	butter	60 mL
1/2 tsp.	salt	2 mL
1/4 tsp.	pepper	1 mL
pinch	tarragon	pinch
2 tbsp.	finely chopped fresh chives	30 mL
4 tbsp.	milk	60 mL
8	eggs, beaten	8
6	slices smoked salmon lox, chopped	6
4	English muffins, split and toasted	4
1/4 lb.	cream cheese	125 g
2 tbsp.	black caviar	30 mL

Combine the butter, salt, pepper, tarragon and chives in a 4-cup (1 L) microproof dish. Microwave on HIGH 100% power 1 minute.

Blend together the milk and eggs. Microwave on MEDIUM 50% power 2 minutes. Stir well and microwave on MEDIUM 50% power in 1 minute increments until eggs are barely set, stirring well after each cooking period. Stir in the lox, reserving about 1 tbsp. (15 mL) for garnish.

Spread toasted English muffin halves with cream cheese and arrange them on a serving platter. Divide eggs evenly among the muffin halves.

Top each portion with a little of the reserved lox and the caviar.

Serve immediately.

The Easy Gourmet features a photograph of this recipe on page 143.

BRUNCH MILANO

For brunch, lunch, buffet, or just a special breakfast, this is a savoury, vitamin-packed dish. Try it with a tart green salad and a basket of warm, crusty rolls. Serves 6.

1 tbsp.	butter	15 mL
1	small clove garlic, crushed	1
1/2 cup	finely chopped green onion	125 mL
4 tbsp.	finely chopped red bell pepper	60 mL
4 tbsp.	finely chopped green bell pepper	60 mL
4 tbsp.	finely chopped celery	60 mL
1/2 cup	sliced mushrooms	125 mL
1 cup	1/4 inch (6 mm) bread cubes	250 mL
1 cup	grated sharp Cheddar cheese	250 mL
1/2 cup	grated Parmesan cheese	125 mL
6	large eggs, lightly beaten	6
1/2 tsp.	salt	2 mL
1/4 tsp.	pepper	1 mL
1	14 oz. (398 mL) can Italian tomato sauce	1

Place the butter, garlic, green onion, green and red peppers, celery and mushrooms in an 8-cup (2 L) microproof dish. Cover and microwave on HIGH 100% power 3-5 minutes until the vegetables are softened, stirring at least once during the cooking time. Mix in the bread cubes and cheeses. Blend the salt and pepper into the beaten eggs and then stir the eggs into the vegetable mixture.

Microwave on MEDIUM 50% power in 2 minute increments until the eggs are just set, moving cooked portions from the edge of the dish to the centre.

Place the tomato sauce in a microproof dish and microwave on HIGH 100% power 2-4 minutes until heated through.

To serve, top each portion of Brunch Milano with tomato sauce.

BAKED EGGS WITH ARTICHOKE SAUCE

Artichokes, cream and curry team up with eggs in this unusual, versatile dish. The perfect accompaniment is fresh seasonal fruit and baguette rounds, crisped in a 300°F (150°C) oven with sweet butter and grated Parmesan cheese. Serves 6.

2 tbsp.	butter	30 mL
4 tbsp.	chopped onion	60 mL
1	14 oz. (398 mL) can artichoke hearts, drained and slivered	1
1/2 tsp.	curry powder	2 mL
4 tbsp.	chicken broth	60 mL
1 cup	half-and-half cream	250 mL
1/2 tsp.	salt	2 mL
dash	white pepper	dash
1/2 tsp.	chopped fresh chervil	2 mL
6	large eggs	6
	whole fresh leaves of chervil for garnish	

Butter six 4 oz. (125 mL) individual ramekin dishes or custard cups with about 1 tbsp. (15 mL) of the butter. Place the remaining butter and the onion in a small microproof dish. Cover and microwave on HIGH 100% power 2-3 minutes until onion is soft. Add the slivered artichokes, reserving a few pieces for the garnish. Blend in the curry powder and chicken broth. Microwave on HIGH 100% power 1-2 minutes until heated through. Purée or press through a sieve. Return to the baking dish and blend in the cream, salt, pepper and chopped chervil.

Break one egg into each ramekin dish. Pierce the membrane of each yolk with a fork. Arrange the dishes in a circle in the microwave. Cover with waxed paper and microwave on MEDIUM 50% power 3-6 minutes until the eggs are barely set. Halfway through the cooking time rotate each dish a half turn.

Allow the dishes to stand, covered. Reheat the sauce on MEDIUM 50% power 2-4 minutes, stirring once during the reheating time. To serve, top each egg with sauce. Garnish with whole chervil leaves and reserved slivered artichokes.

LACK FOREST SOUFFLÉ

Soufflés can't wait, so serve this airy creation immediately after it is cooked. While it rises in the oven, toss up a salad and slice some French bread to go with it. And if you just want a light supper for two, this recipe halves beautifully, baked in a 5 cup (1.25 L) soufflé dish. Serves 4.

3 tbsp.	margarine or butter	45 mL
2	shallots, chopped fine	2
3 tbsp.	all-purpose flour	45 mL
1 tbsp.	Dijon mustard	15 mL
1 1/4 cups	milk	300 mL
1 cup	grated Swiss cheese	250 mL
1/3 cup	grated Parmesan cheese	75 mL
1/2 tsp.	salt	2 mL
1/4 tsp.	pepper	1 mL
6	large eggs, separated, at room temperature	6
4 oz. (1 cup)	Black Forest ham, cut in small julienne strips	125 g (250 mL)

Heat the oven to 375°F (190°C). In a medium saucepan, melt the margarine and sauté the shallots about 2 minutes, until soft but not brown. Stir in the flour and cook, stirring, over low heat for 30 seconds. Remove from the heat, stir in the mustard and gradually pour in the milk, stirring constantly. Return to medium heat and bring to a boil, stirring, until the mixture thickens. Turn the heat to low and cook, stirring 2 minutes. Remove from the heat, beat in the Swiss cheese, the Parmesan cheese (reserve about 1 tbsp. [15 mL]), salt and pepper and allow it to cool, stirring occasionally.

Butter a 2 1/2 quart (2.5 L) soufflé dish and sprinkle in the reserved Parmesan cheese to coat the bottom and sides of the dish. In a large bowl, beat the egg yolks. Beat them into the cooled sauce, stir in the ham, then return the mixture to the bowl. In another large bowl, beat the egg whites until stiff. Fold them carefully into the sauce mixture. Pour the mixture into the soufflé dish and bake until well risen and golden brown on top, about 40 minutes. Do not open the oven door while the soufflé cooks, or it will fall.

RAINBOW RIGATONI WITH FOUR CHEESES

Rigatoni—macaroni in a corkscrew shape—is available fresh or dried in convenient packages. Coloured with vegetable dyes, it is a bright dish for a dark day. A creamy sauce of milk, eggs and four tasty cheeses makes this the best macaroni and cheese your family ever had. Serves 4.

1	12 oz. (350 g) pkg. tri-coloured rigatoni, fresh or dried	1
2 tbsp.	butter	30 mL
2 tbsp.	all-purpose flour	30 mL
1 cup	milk	250 mL
1	egg yolk, beaten	1
2 tbsp.	Gruyère or Swiss cheese	30 mL
2 tbsp.	whipping cream	30 mL
	freshly ground pepper and nutmeg	
4 tbsp.	*each* grated yellow Cheddar and grated mozzarella cheese	60 mL
4 tbsp.	grated Parmesan cheese	30 mL
	sprig of parsley or other green herb for garnish	

In a large pot of boiling water, cook the rigatoni *al dente* (just firm to bite), about 3-5 minutes for fresh pasta and 20 minutes for dried. Drain it in a colander by shaking it well. Do not rinse.

Meanwhile, make the sauce. In a medium saucepan, melt the butter. Whisk in the flour and cook for 1 minute. Whisk in the milk and cook, whisking, until the mixture thickens and bubbles. Remove from the heat and whisk a little of the hot mixture into the egg yolk. Return the egg yolk mixture to the saucepan and whisk again. Cook for 1 minute. Add the Gruyère cheese and cream and let cool. Season to taste with pepper and nutmeg.

When ready to serve, reheat the sauce to almost boiling. Place the rigatoni in a large bowl and pour the sauce over it. Toss to mix well. Spoon servings onto plates and top each with a generous sprinkling of the three remaining cheeses. Garnish with parsley or other fresh herb.

VERNIGHT CHEESE PUFF

Prepared the night before and popped into the oven for breakfast, this fragrant, puffy dish calls for freshly squeezed orange juice and a colourful platter of fresh seasonal fruits. Serves 6.

15	slices enriched white bread, crusts removed	15
	(save for the crumb topping)	
1/2 lb.	sharp Cheddar cheese, grated	250 g
6	large eggs	6
4 cups	milk	1 L
1 1/2 tbsp.	salt	25 mL
1 1/2 tsp.	Worcestershire sauce	7 mL
1/4 tsp.	dry mustard	1 mL
	freshly ground black pepper	

Cube the bread and crumble the crusts, reserving the crumbs for topping. Layer the bread with the cheese in a large flat casserole, 9 x 13 inches (23 x 32 cm). Beat together the remaining ingredients and pour over the cheese and bread. Press the bread down to absorb the liquid. Refrigerate overnight. Heat the oven to 350°F (180°C). Sprinkle on the reserved crumbs and bake until puffy and browned, about 1 hour.

Bits of ham, sausage or chile peppers can be added to taste. Or try slivers of tomatoes, red or green bell pepper, etc., added halfway through the baking time.

Serve immediately, when the dish is hot and puffed.

CANADIAN WHITE CHEDDAR RAREBIT

Serve this hearty, satisfying, famous cheese dish—this one unique in its use of Canadian white sharp Cheddar—ladled over buttered and toasted crumpets. Serve several slices of crispy streaky bacon and broiled red ripe tomatoes alongside. The perfect beverage is icy beer or ale, or chilled apple cider. Garnish with thin slivers of crisp apple, and serve piping hot. Serves 4.

6 tbsp.	butter, softened	90 mL
1 tsp.	English-style dry mustard	5 mL
8	crumpets or English muffins, split	8
12 oz.	sharp white Cheddar cheese; 3 cups (750 mL) grated	375 g
1/2 cup	beer, ale, dry apple cider or non-alcoholic beer	125 mL
1 tsp.	prepared English-style hot mustard	5 mL
	large pinch cayenne pepper	
	salt to taste	
	pinch paprika	

In a small bowl, combine 4 tbsp. (60 mL) of the softened butter and dry mustard. Divide, and spread over the crumpets or muffins. Place the crumpets on a cookie sheet and, watching carefully, broil 8 inches (20 cm) from heat until golden brown and bubbly. Remove and keep warm. Coarsely grate the cheese.

In a heavy, deep saucepan combine the grated cheese, beer (or ale or cider) and butter. Over low heat, cook, stirring constantly, until the cheese is melted and the sauce is very smooth. Stir in the prepared mustard and cayenne. Season to taste with salt, and whisk smooth and creamy.

To assemble: On warmed plates, place 2 toasted crumpets per portion. Ladle over them the warm cheese rarebit, and top with a pinch of paprika for colour. Serve at once with 2-3 crispy bacon rashers, broiled tomatoes, and thin slices of apple.

B LUE CHEESE, LEEK AND NUT QUICHE

If you enjoy the full-bodied taste of blue cheese mixed with crunchy nuts, here is a new flavour twist on the traditional French quiche. This is a deep dish pie, so make your own shell or save time by buying a prepared shell from the frozen pastry section. A crunchy, bright green salad is the ideal accompaniment. Serves 6.

1	9-inch (23 cm) deep dish unbaked pastry pie shell	1
3	strips bacon, chopped	3
2 cups	sliced leeks, washed	500 mL
1/2 cup	crumbled Danish blue cheese	125 mL
1/2 cup	toasted chopped pecans or walnuts	125 mL
2	large eggs	2
1 cup	half-and-half cream	250 mL
	salt and pepper	

Heat the oven to 425°F (220°C). Prick the bottom of the pastry lightly with a fork. Line it with foil and bake it on a cookie sheet for 10 minutes. Remove the foil and bake for a further 3 minutes. Remove and cool. Reduce the oven temperature to 350°F (180°C).

Fry the bacon in a skillet until crisp. Remove with a slotted spoon and sprinkle over the bottom of the pie shell. Pour off all but 1 tbsp. (15 mL) of the fat from the skillet and fry the leeks over medium heat for 3 minutes or until just soft. Sprinkle the leeks over the bacon, adding the cheese and pecans.

In a medium bowl, beat together the eggs, cream, salt and pepper. Pour the mixture into the pastry shell. Bake until the filling is golden and doesn't jiggle, 35 to 40 minutes.

The Easy Gourmet features a photograph of this recipe on page 143.

INDEX